Sleeping With the Fish

New and Collected Works

by Catfish McDaris

Copyright © 2016 by Catfish McDaris

Layout: Pski's Porch
Cover design: Pski's Porch
Cover art: Jeff Alfier
Back cover art: Anonymous

All rights reserved. No part of this book may be reproduced in any form by any electronic or mechanical means including photocopying, recording, or information storage and retrieval without permission in writing from the author.

ISBN-13: 978-0692671320
ISBN-10: 0692671323

for more books, visit Pski's Porch:
www.pskisporch.com

Printed in U.S.A

"Wild Bukowski-esque tales and poetry. Great juxtaposition between poems and short stories." *Antler*

"You're a master dude with the short story." *Ron Androla, editor Translucent Tendency Press*

"McDaris rages at the society which reared him. These pomz are filled w/angst & they spit at you." *Patrick McKinnon, editor of North Coast Review & Poetry Motel*

"Caution: Van Gogh's Ear, may rattle your windows. From a mighty mouth of Milwaukee." *Miles Grenadier, editor of Ignis Fatuus in Bisbee, AZ and inventor of the talking poetic watch*

"Van Gogh's Ear kicked my motherfucking ass!" *Al Rogovin, editor of Girder in New Jersey*

Contents

La Tristesse Durera Toujours	13
Riding the Bear	14
Carnage	15
Mexican Dominoes	16
The Duke's Hoss	17
Lala	18
Isla Mujeres	19
The Sky Was Larger Than Australia and Africa Having Mad Sex	20
Skinny Dogs and Spotted Horses	21
Phombies	22
The Wig Shop Blues	23
Gophers Are Heathens	25
Blue Frankenstein	26
The Three Bears	29
Laughing Cockroach	30
The Giraffe That Jumped Over the Moon	31
Coozeman	36
Oceans of Purple	38
Brain Cells to Burn	40
Apache Dream Lady	41
Green around the Gills	42
Lady Death	44
Cambodia	46
The Bricklayer	47
The Jig	48
Cooking Dead Stuff	49
Gringo Tacos	50
Blowing the Dog	51
Spaghettio Capone	52
The Most Beautiful Lady in Albuquerque	54
The Asteroid	58
A Sea Of Mermaids	60
Nevuary	62
The Magic Rabbit	68

Jail Roping	69
Zupidx	70
The North Pole Blues	71
Chicken Foot Soup	72
Making Love to the Rain	74
It's Getting Hard as I Write	75
Respect	76
Maria Takes a Powder	79
Baked Alaska	84
Black Knife	86
Romeo Van Gogh	96
Frida Kahlo	98
The Same Rifle That Killed JFK	102
Hippopotamus Summer	103
Pluck	104
The Ants	105
Defacing the Mail	106
Hot Pussy	108
Under the Atlantic	109
Juarez, Mexico	111
Hazel Blue Rat Malaria	113
Eating Raw Jackrabbit and Snorting Black Cocaine	115
Last Comanchero of Dildo Island	117
Little Vietnam, Tigerland Fort Polk, Louisiana	121
Lipstick on a Pig	125
Water	129
Mermaids and Gila Monsters	131
Picasso Left with Elvis	132
A Dirt Nap	133
Peanut Dreams	134
Hombre Lobo	135
Too Much Tabasco	136
Phuque Book	137
A Coma in Oklahoma	138
Going Postal	139
Nestled In the Paloverde	141

Hiding in My Wounds	143
How I Pulled the Rabbit Out of the Hat	144
Bring Me an Apple with No Worms	148
Mamasita Mambo	149
Jackalope Condoms	151
A Geronimo Moon	154
Next Time	158
The Trade	159
Soldier	160
Brujo	162
Tiger Skin Blues	163
Porcupine Ice Cream	164
Throwing Curve Balls	166
Defying Logic and Gravity	168
The Perverts	169
Pussy Man in Paris	171
The Last Night Shift	173
War Everyday Everywhere War Everyday	174
Everywhere	174
The Man That Slept With Verbal Hand Grenades Under His Pillow	176
Left Hook Tony	178
I Hope that's Pepperoni	180
Czarnina Thieves	181
The Good, The Bad, and The Ugly	182
A NYC Salute	184
Walk It If You Talk It	185
Gone Amazon	186
Soldier Blues	187
Dreaming of Paris	188
She Loved Me Because Of Poetry	189
Howling at the Ginsberg Moon	191
Speedy Gonzales	192
Four Beers a Day	193
Spanish Harlem	195
Honeymoon at Viagra Falls	196
The First Car I Wrecked	197

Eating Televisions	198
My Penis Has No Brain	199
Nirvana Blues	200
The Revolution of Love	201
the wino and the mermaid	202
Sky Pilots	203
Chiapas Lie	205
The Gordian Knot	206
The Grape Cigar	207
Noise	208
Moose Jaw Blues	209
Amarillo	210
Five Finger Discount	212
Crime in Milwaukee	214
It Only Hurts When He Cracks a Smile	216
The Sky Was Larger Than Los Angeles and New York City Having Mad Sex	217
The Last Poem	218
The Panhandle	220
Five Times Faster Than Sound	221
The Blues Jumped Up and Bit Him in the Ass	222
Onions Make Me Cry	223
The Fortune Cookie	224
Dancing With the Queen of Hearts	225
Electric Ladyland	226
Nasty Monkey	227
Rasputin's Hedgehogs	228
Dead Butterflies in the Snow	229
While My Raging Typer Bleeds	230
The City of Perverts	231
All You'll Ever Want	232
Sandman Blues	233
The Eighth Deadly Sin	234
Sound of the Sunrise	235
When Later Never Comes	236
The Margarita Machine	237

Felony Littering	238
Boom Boom Lil	240
The Ass That Wouldn't Quit	242
Gringo Loco	244
Never Eat Barbequed Seagulls	245
Supernatural	246
The Tumbleweed	247
Elephant Tusk Boogie	248
Six Headed Dog	249
Masturbating In a Straitjacket	250
On Top of Old Smokey	252
Crying From One Eye	253
No Blindfold No Cigarette	254
Making the Meat Go Farther	255
Quicksand	256
Eating Dog Without Salt	258
Christmas in Milwaukee	259
Adolf and Elton	260
The One Eared Dutchman	261
Acknowledgements	263

La Tristesse Durera Toujours
The Sadness Will Last Forever

Quick was born a chubby slimy snot near a prairie dog town on Route 66. His old man pulled over his 48 Chevy with his ma screaming holy murder in the backseat. Some Navajo women stopped and helped with his delivery. All of them shaking their heads in disbelief at all seventeen pounds of Quick. A state trooper directed traffic around his dad and the two families from Gallup. Growing up he always had strange ideas, Quick disliked school or work, but had a gift of gab for the ladies. His ma entered raffles. She won a year's supply of toilet paper, seven ant farms, a pogo stick, 52 box kites, some old expired Jimmy Dean sausage, and lots of other strange stuff. His pa just let her live in her own little world, cutting coupons and collecting green and gold stamps. He built things from stone and drank Smirnoff 100 proof vodka, Ten Roses whiskey, and Coors beer. Quick practiced Spanish, so he could disappear into Mexico and eventually deal weed. Quick always loved to write down his thoughts, which led him to stories and poems. Like yesterday he saw this poor dumb son of a bitch in the grocery store wearing an Elmer Fudd hunting cap. In his shopping basket he had 4 cans of chili with beans (real fart blasters), air freshener (that would never cut the stench), a roll of cheap ass toilet paper (that wouldn't fit in the wall dispenser and would leave shit and dingle balls up his butt), a jar of Vaseline (stroke action), and a Penthouse (at least he got one thing right). It made him think about Van Gogh, he may not have sold a painting while he was alive, but his last words were right on the money. "La tristesse durera toujours."

Riding the Bear

Quick was waiting for a northbound bus in front of the Taco Bell. A young dude with goatee and baseball cap askew in rusty Pontiac bucket of bolt goosed the gas. The rotted muffler was held up with coat hangers and had seen better days. The smooth operator was sucking on a Swisher Sweet cigar, Quick used to smoke them while fishing. Pontiac boy said, "Hey, if you weren't so poor, you wouldn't be riding the bus." Then he shot him the finger and blew a smoke ring. Quick just smiled and blew him a kiss. He looked up the street and didn't see the bus, so he crossed over and bought a cup of coffee from a gas station. Finger boy made the block and almost flattened Quick's foot. "What did you mean by blowing me a kiss, old man?" Quick showed him how he got his nickname. He reached in with mongoose lightning swiftness and grabbed a handful of hair and started honking the horn with his face. Then he jerked him through the window and shined his combat boots on his butt. Quick retrieved his coffee from the top of a gas pump. "Your car might be on North Avenue, unless I donate it to the poor." Quick tossed him a bus ticket and drove away laughing.

Carnage

All his life Quick heard bizarre rumors about his father. He remembered the tiny town in Oklahoma where his father was from. There were oil wells everywhere, even right in the middle of Main St. The wells resembled metal Pterodactyls sucking up black dinosaur blood. Johnny, Quick's dad was wounded nineteen times by Japanese machinegun fire in World War 2. Lucky for him they had run out of lead and had to use wood projectiles. Johnny's legs and buttocks looked like chunks of raw hamburger. He caught malaria on the Bataan Death March in the Philippines. Every six months, he'd go into a bad spell trance. Quick loved him and used to make up stories about him. He said, "Time stood still for the man that didn't sleep. You could cheat death in a game of Texas Hold 'em and the gold will keep stacking up, until the table legs get weak. Sometimes after these lies I tell, my tongue grows so long I bite it bloody while trying to eat." Then he'd take an afternoon siesta. Once Quick woke up in a canyon valley full of extinct creatures. The earth tremble like it was in agony. A Tyrannosaurus Rex was eating a Brontosaurus like a steam shovel scooping bloody coal into its gigantic mouth. There were roars from all four directions. Two Triceratops were goring each other with entrails streaming red carnage on their hooked heads. Quick had to escape this sleep induced madness. He leaped onto the back of a flying Quetzalcoatlus. They flew out of the ravine high into the snow covered mountains.

Mexican Dominoes

Playing dominoes, sipping cerveza, and smoking Cubanos in Mexico City was heaven for Quick. His lady, Rosita's Uncle and Aunt had a huge house next to the old bullfighting ring. During the bullfighting season you could hear the yelling of ole and you had to watch out for pickpockets, it was said the thieves could steal your socks while your shoes were on. Tio Luis would have the dominoes ready for a game. Tia Carmen and her beautiful daughters would take Rosita to the kitchen for gossip and cooking lessons. Theresa, one of Carmen's daughters was a famous television star. All of the women were very easy on the eyes. Luis and Quick would play the bones until late in the afternoon. All the children would leave and Rosita and Quick would go to the guest room in the former servant's quarters. Carmen would usually nap over her sewing machine and Luis would nod off on the couch. That's when the fireworks would start. Carmen would fart real loud, then Luis would answer her fart with a louder one of his own. This fart barrage went on, while Rosita had her hand clamped over Quick's mouth to keep him from exploding with laughter. Finally Luis woke up with ferocious ass boom. Carmen replied with a brutal pucker up and squeeze monster that seemed to fly around the room and bang on all four walls. Luis yelled, "Hey woman, go answer the door. Someone is knocking for you."

The Duke's Hoss

The Mexican told Quick about working for the Duke down in Acapulco. He told him some Asians were the main servants. How the Duke liked to get his peter unloaded on regular intervals. Pussy was never a problem, but he liked feeling the power of pulling some guy's ears while, blowing his load into their mouth. One day the Chinamen picked the wrong motherfucker for a blowjob, Loco Louie. He damn near bit that movie star's pecker right off down to the nuts. They fucked up Loco real good. That was a big mistake not killing him. He snuck in one night and bit the dick off the Duke's prize stallion. Loco cut the horse dick in half. He shoved half down the Duke's throat and the stuck the rest up his ass.

Lala

Quick's sister Roberta had a girlfriend called Lala. She was a big girl, but always smiling and laughing. The laughter seemed to fill her eyes and sparkle onto everyone she met. Quick was fascinated, enthralled, and thoroughly captivated. Lala was an outstanding cook, her specialty was Mexican food. She made goat burritos and pig brain enchiladas that were out of this universe delicious. Roberta was happy that Quick paid so much attention to her friend, but at the same time she was afraid he would break her heart. Lala kept growing in girth and eventually passed the 400 pound mark. Her doctor put a device in her stomach and she started dropping weight rapidly. On the down side she cut some wicked smelly farts while dieting, even Quick had to get nose plugs and safety goggles because his eyes watered so tremendously. In less than a year Lala was under 200 pounds. She got surgery to tighten her skin. Her farts went away slowly. Everything seemed to be going swell, but then she got a coon dog and named him Beauregard. Lala loved that dog, she would take him for long walks with Quick tagging along. The dog took monster shits, Lala would ask Quick to pick up the turds in plastic bag to dispose of. He wasn't happy about this. Lala called him a pussy. Soon she was picking up the dog shit with her bare hand. Quick said fuck this noise. Roberta said she understood, but Quick had his doubts.

Isla Mujeres

Sometimes Quick couldn't tell if he was chasing ghosts or if the ideas he had were feasible. He left his woman, Lala after she got stone ass crazy. He referred to her as the last best piece of ass on earth or Satan incarnate. Quick drifted through the mountains in Mexico, exploring ruins and Mayan pyramids. He fished in the ocean, rivers, and lakes. Cooking and eating on the beach with the smiling people of the south land. Quick learned to scuba dive and looked for treasure and pearls. He heard about a sunken airplane in Quintana Roo off the Yucatan coast in Cozumel. Living expenses were cheap and Quick had put together enough money to live easy for a while. The island of Cozumel was paradise and not far away was Isla Mujeres, where Europeans, mostly French sunbathed nude. Quick rented a motor scooter and found a small zoo with a palm thatch roofed bar. There was an aquarium and fish tanks, mostly filled with red snapper. The cooks wrapped the fish in banana leaves and rubbed garlic and chili and oregano and threw them on a smoky grill. The beer was icy cold and the tequila served with lime and salt was excellent. The best thing was the floor show. There was a monkey tethered on a rope in nest in a coconut tree, eating boiled eggs. When the tourist buses stopped the monkey would climb down and snatch off the lady's bikini tops and bottoms and grab their purse and throw their money and stuff all over the place. They would be standing there naked trying to gather their money and credit cards. Laughter turned into tears and tears turned into laughter.

The Sky Was Larger Than Australia and Africa Having Mad Sex

After the 1902 sardine shortage, Quick knew he could no longer make a living fishing, so he sold his boat and fish canning factory. He drifted west and started painting. At first he stuck with landscapes, birds, and experiments, before he went on to draw and paint people. When he got to the Pacific Ocean, there seemed to be pink marijuana clouds above Malibu. The salt air made him long for his old life, it was simple and clean. Over Tanqueray martinis, Quick watched the Angelinos, they danced as they walked, smooth and cool. He met a beautiful senorita, named Juanita, her body seemed eager, but peril lurked deep in her brown eyes. Quick drew her with a look of wanton pleasure on her face. From his sketch, he made a beautiful painting and showed it to her. Juanita was mad and embarrassed at first, but the painting was so erotic and flattering it aroused her. He persuaded her to move in with him. Their apartment was made with adobe blocks and had viga post roof beams. It was soon filled with smoky chipotles, cilantro, tortillas, and delicious Mexican cooking aromas. She posed for him, at first clothed, then nude. They seduced each other as if every day was their last. They made galaxy shattering love knocking paintings off the walls, tipping over vases of Alcatraz flowers, scaring alley cats. Lightning and whirlwinds seemed to fill their adobe house. Capturing Juanita like a tiger gone mad, at the height of orgasmic desire, was what he finally succeeded at. He kept a fish hook and line is his pocket for luck and so he knew they would never go hungry. Quick dreamed often of a French stockbroker that quit his life and went to Tahiti, but he'd found his home it was in the eyes of Juanita.

Skinny Dogs and Spotted Horses

Quick traded a Bowie knife and an Arkansas toothpick for a cayuse with brown clouds across its white rump. The horse looked strong and knew how to dance and fly. Quick harnessed a rope bridle and threw an old Mexican saddle blanket over her. The horse galloped so fast, he thought his skin was peeling back like a shedding snake. Quick rode back to the stable for his gear and the skinny black dog that he'd been giving scraps to, followed them out of town. The first night they camped under some cottonwood trees, he had some grain and there was scrub grass for the horse. He stirred up a pot of coffee and made some venison stew, throwing the dog some deer jerky. The stars were happy and making love in the sky. Then the dog started farting and the horse must've felt challenged. The: who stepped on the bullfrog contest, was on. Quick moved his bedroll back from the fire, he didn't feel like getting all his hair singed off in case of explosion.

Phombies

Cell phone madness was driving the world insane. People walking into things, holding phones up to the side of their heads, blue gadgets stuck in their ears, finger stabbing on tiny keyboards. Folks not speaking to one another, only concerned with electronic communications. Families sitting down for a meal, each and every one of them ignoring each other caught up in their own personal world. Quick warned his daughter to slow down with all her cell phone usage. He explained his theory about phones consuming all human intelligence and conquering the world. Quick's kid, just shook her head like her old man was hopelessly behind the times. A few days later Quick went to wake his child up, her head was covered by sheets and blankets. When she finally struggled to get up, she had no head. From the neck up was a cell phone. He yelled for his wife and they went berserk, they tried to talk to their kid, but got no response. Quick's wife sent her a text and it appeared on her face phone. They called an ambulance and reported the incident. They were informed that Phombism was a wide spread virus. There were laboratories and hospitals working on a cure, but all cell phones must be confiscated and destroyed, before a useable vaccine could be developed to treat the Phombies. Quick looked out the window and saw people with cell phone heads stumbling down the street. It was utter chaos, he went to the refrigerator and poured a glass of buttermilk.

The Wig Shop Blues

Financial situations can be a sickening rollercoaster rides. Pockets flush one moment, a wallet full of nothing the next. Quick had worked his ass off at a vast array of jobs before settling into a post office job. He only got that job because he was an army veteran during the Vietnam War and he was excellent with numbers. Veterans got extra point on the postal exam, so he scored high on the test. Quick worked for years on nights with bad off days, split shifts, every holiday, and every day in December for the Christmas rush for over thirty years. He finally got weekends off with a noon start, then they bombarded him with mandatory overtime. After thirty four years, he retired. Five years later, they cut his pension in half and told him he had to take three quarters of his Social Security benefits. Quick thought about doing some banks, but had no desire for prison. He decided he had no choice, he had to find a job. Over the years Quick had worn his body down, like a horse ridden hard and put up wet. He called up a Korean pal that owned a wig shop and asked for a job. He'd known Kwong for thirty years and Kwong told him, he'd try him out part time. The wig shop was in a dangerous neighborhood. It seemed most of the clientele were African-American ladies. They wanted extensions, weaves, and wigs of all sorts. The black women dressed nice and drove big fine cars. Kwong's beautiful wife, sister-in-law, and a few cousins worked there. After Quick learned the basics of wig sales, many of the clients preferred to buy from him. The Koreans ate lots of garlic with every meal, their breath was terribly awful. Quick had gotten used to it over the years from working with them. On Quick's second day of work, a lady dropped her purse and out rolled a 45 automatic, the safety wasn't on. He snatched it off the floor, put it on safe, unloaded it, and gave it back to the lady. He made friends with the ladies buying wigs and they had friends coming in often.

After six weeks, Quick asked to be put on commission instead of working by the hour. Kwong's wife, Hai wasn't happy with this suggestion. There was another wig store two blocks down the street, Quick took a walk at lunch and spoke with the manager. Hai started treating Quick like the godfather of Seoul and he danced all the way to the bank.

Gophers Are Heathens

Quick's daughter recently graduated from college. They had a big party and she got lots of envelopes. His holy roller Aunt came with his cousin, Quick had grown up with. Right away his cousin started passing out religious pamphlets. He asked her if she wanted a cheeseburger, she said yes. Quick sprinkled habanero flakes on it and his Aunt's. She kept talking about God, until she bit into that burger. Nobody could believe she was related to him. His Aunt checked her food and got an Italian sausage for herself. She started quizzing Quick's kid about her degree and how her boyfriend was a decorated veteran. She said she kept a loaded pistol by the toilet and another by her bed. How she'd been sitting on the pot in the dark and how their Uncle came into pee and she almost blew his nuts off. That sure brought a lull to the conversation. Aunt then told about their cousin's kids killing gophers with a sledge hammer. People were aghast. She said gophers don't have souls. Then Quick remembered why they hadn't gone over to dinner or spoken in seven years.

Blue Frankenstein

Jesus Quick gobbled baby food like a starving goat. His mother tried to burp him, but he cut loose with some strong stinky loud farts. His father, Jesus Senior was a large construction worker, he laid bricks and could build just about anything. When his mom gave the baby to him, he patted him on the back and the stench damn near choked the old man. His dad started calling him, Fart Baby. Sometimes appropriate nicknames stick for life. They would go grocery shopping and if anyone bothered them or was rude, they'd aim Fart Baby's little lethal ass at them and he'd fire away like a cannon. Jesus Quick curled eyebrows, made strong men want to puke, made women scream, and made people scatter. His parents took Fart Baby to the doctor, he said he'll probably grow out of it. That never happened, he just got worse. Quick's teachers refused to call him his nickname and weren't too happy about calling him Jesus, so they settled on Quick. He ate lots of frijoles, corn and tortillas, which multiplied his ass power greatly. He could fart on demand and learned many tricks with his potent ass. Ventriloquism was a specialty, he could make a fart come from his teacher at the blackboard which would crack up entire his class. He made cops fart, the priest in church, nuns, and his mom, anybody he took a dislike to. He learned to use the silent but deadly method. Quick could squeak like a dying mouse or rabbit, he could make bird calls, sound like a howling coyote. He filled balloons with fart gas sold them to his friends as stink bombs to go. Every day he learned new tricks and he became quite versatile. The only thing he lacked was girlfriends, but once he mastered his butt that changed. Quick had lots of pals. They all worked on the brick jobs with his father as laborers and hod carriers. Reefer was his best pal, he smoked lots of weed. Fucking Aye got his name from not talking much other than saying, fucking aye a lot. Right On was a young soul brother that was

Popsicle cool. Quick was soon given a brick trowel and he was slapping bricks and stone into mortar. He liked working in the open air, so he could practice farting without too much complaint. Jesus Sr. hired three masons from Mexico and at lunch, they'd build a little fire and warm beans and chorizo. Quick loved to eat with them, but he'd cut loose with some ungodly farts. The three Chavez brothers told him he should become an exterminator with his ass. They planted the seed of an idea. Reefer used to complain about washing his car all the time, one day he drove up in a patch work velour car. It was an old Plymouth all green, blue, red, orange, and purple with rust peeking through. It looked like someone had puked on it after a Hawaiian luau. He'd gone to a second hand store and bought up lots of old fake velvet shirts and dresses and glued them all over his car. We were all waiting for the first rain and hail storm to see how his idea panned out. Reefer passed around a bong with some serious stink weed. Right On did a funky chicken alligator dance on the hood, Fucking Aye just grinned and said fucking aye. Quick laughed through tears until his old man said work time hombres. Fucking Aye mixed a new batch of mortar after Right On did the walk like an Egyptian while cleaning a wheelbarrow. Quick and his buddies started scoring Acapulco gold at a snooker hall near Albuquerque. It was forty dollars per kilo and came up from Mexico hidden in railroad box cars. Quick had always used his brain for business. He bought two pinball machines, set them up in his parent's garage and charged all the kids a nickel a game. He bought three electric lawnmowers with long extension cords from Montgomery Ward's and started a lawn service business. Quick bought some pigs and raised them for pork, feeding them for free from expired store produce. He used the pig shit for fertilizer for his fourteen foot tall marijuana plants in Tucumcari. Reefer and him harvested the weed and loaded it in the Reefer Mobile and found a place to dry it. One night Quick's parents weren't home, he had a small party. The cops broke down the front door, but only found some beer, Reefer and Right On had swallowed the joint they had rolled. The cops tore up the house looking for their stash. They took Quick to jail, he stunk up their car and jail so bad, they regretted that decision. Jesus Sr. got him out of the pokey, he told the Chief of Police to stay the fuck away from his son. Reefer came over a few days later and they moved twenty kilos of Mexican gold tops and five gunny sacks of home grown from Quick's cottonwood tree house. Quick got one letter from Vietnam from Right On. It said, he'd made corporal and he'd tell all his men to get down and they'd all stand up and start dancing and get wasted. A month later Right On's mom told him, he'd been killed. Fucking Aye and Reefer went to Mexico. Quick got arrested for marijuana and was given a choice of jail or the army, he chose being a soldier for Uncle Sam for three years. That prison up in Santa Fe didn't like white boys, even if they knew Spanish. They closed the book on Vietnam and Quick ended up in Germany, most of the time at the same base as Elvis Presley. Lots of good beer, wine, hash, and ladies, when he wasn't blasting his eardrums shooting howitzer cannons in the cold war games, school was in session. Later in life, Quick would realize getting an honorable discharge from the army was one of his greatest and most important achievements, even if it was signed by Richard M. Nixon.

The Three Bears

A ferocious bear jumped out of a tree onto Quick's shoulder, he was riding Brown Hand his Comanche horse. Quick tried to sling the bear off, but its claws were sunk into his shoulders. If the bear got its teeth into his neck, that would be all she wrote. Brown Hand bucked against a big fir tree and his dog, Killer a scrawny black mutt was able to distract the bear enough, so Quick could get to his knife. He had a long wicked razor sharp blade, he slipped into the bear's mouth before it could make an omelet of his brains. Quick cut the bear open all the way down its chest, a wolverine jumped out of its guts. It tried to rape Killer, Quick pulled his hog leg and emptied 44's into its eyeballs. There was a creek nearby, so he could get moss and medicinal plants for a poultice for their wounds. Quick was just happy Brown Hand and Killer weren't injured too seriously. That night they ate bear and wolverine stew. Brown Hand had some grain and wild apples. Two days later, another bear leaped from a tree, Brown Hand must've smelled him. She reared her front hooves high into the air and knocked the bear into a swamp. Killer and Quick looked on as a herd of alligators swarmed that bear like angry cannibal flies. In moments it was just a pile of fur and blood. A week later they made it to the Porcupine Mountains and another bear leaped from a tree. Quick, Brown Hand, and Killer were tired of bears attacking. Quick was ready to murder this bear, when the bear started talking. It said, "Please kind sir don't kill me, I am really a beautiful woman. A witch put a spell on me, turning me into a bear. If you kiss me I can turn back into a lady and I will grant you three wishes. Plus I'll be your sex slave forever. What do say?" Quick thought why not. He kissed the bear and waited for the transformation. The bear changed into a blonde lady with sparkling blue eyes, but she kept growing and growing. Soon she was a giant, she bent down and crushed and swallowed Brown Hand, Killer, and Quick. Then she turned into an aardvark and disappeared into the forest.

Laughing Cockroach

Sunlight sliced the clouds like a tomahawk, people were frying eggs and bacon on the hoods of their cars. Quick was hustling shoes, but lady luck was unhappy. He ducked into a dive bar to wet his whistle. It was cool and smoky, in the shadows there appeared to be some unusual clientele. He ordered a draft and opened his case. A few of the patrons moseyed over. Quick took out a matchbox and out came a huge cockroach. The bartender grabbed a flyswatter, but Quick held him at bay. The cockroach started singing, Hotel California and dancing. Then he performed a few flips and dove into a shot of rye whiskey. Quick asked if anybody would like to buy a pair of shoes. Nobody said anything, so he put the bug back in the matchbox, packed his case and split. He got a few feet out the door and a man caught up with him. He said he'd like to buy the cockroach for a thousand dollars. Quick agreed, he counted the money and gave him a matchbox with a roach. They got in their El Camino and Quick let the magic cockroach out, they both laughed.

The Giraffe That Jumped Over the Moon

Dr. Danny Quick used the last of his Jimi Hendrix stamps to mail off his manuscript to California. He hoped Jimi would bring his screenplay good luck. It was Ernest Hemingway's birthday, Quick often thought about Santiago the Cuban fisherman that never gave up. That's how he felt sometimes about his writing. Quick decided he needed a change of scenery, he wanted to live on the moon. All these rich people were flying into outer space, all it took was greed, power, and big money.

Space travel had advanced at a rapid pace. Settling on the moon in geodesic domes was no longer just a dream. The first trial dome was soon to be inhabited by six different nations. Spacecraft from each nation would blast off, each carrying six astronauts with supplies and material to build the habitat. There were plants that would produce oxygen and water would be recycled from the moon's surface where asteroids and comets hit in the Grail rift valleys.

Earth had too many people. Diseases had been mostly eradicated. People were living longer due to better medicines. Food was easily produced. Birth control wasn't practiced to the degree necessary, so the planet had finally reached its capacity. The world's leaders united to discuss solutions to this drastic problem. The six governments sending three men and women each, needed qualified candidates to represent them on the moon. This would be the biggest joint venture in space, mankind had ever endeavored. All thirty six astronauts must exemplify high intelligence and stamina.

Dr. Quick had degrees in astrophysics, mechanical engineering, and paleontology. He spoke four languages fluently and had lived in many different countries growing up and as an adult. Quick could fix anything and he was in excellent physical condition from Tai Chi and martial arts. His name was on the space program list to be considered for living on the moon for six months.

Quick never cared about money, he was concerned about answers to his questions. Since the meteorite ALH84001 from Mars was discovered with fossils of diatoms. This required further investigation and Dr. Quick was intrigued. There had been rumors in the scientific community that ancient giraffe fossils had been discovered on the moon. Quick had no absolute confirmation of this remarkable discovery. He'd been studying the gaping theory in Charles Darwin's The Origin of Species claiming that a horse like animal converted into a giraffe due to the need to eat from higher tree branches. The Okapi was the ancestor and migrated to feed.

Paleontologists were split into many different groups on the theories about the Sivatherius fossils being from giraffes with a trunk like an elephant. Some scientist believed the giraffe came from a Samotherium from the late Miocene era or 14.6 million years ago. Dr. Quick had participated in an isotope fractionation tests for fossils. Some thought the origins of life could be buried in lava flows on the moon. If a lunar regolith was conducted and organic molecules remained intact, there was no reason why fossils shouldn't be found on the moon. Quick had studied the knowledge of the Babylonians, the Nubians, and the Chinese about dark matter and dark energy. His vast computer-like mind held information about gamma ray bursts, cosmic microwave radiation, the Magellanic Cloud, and the Andromeda Galaxy. Quick had flown airplanes, jets, and helicopters for many years. He'd worked for NASA and had almost gone to space, he was over qualified if anything. He was just waiting for the next mission into outer space.

Dr. Quick arrived in Antarctica to aid in the examination of ALH84001 the Martian meteorite. The temperatures there could reach -129 Fahrenheit, it was 98% ice. It was the coldest, driest, windiest, highest average elevation continent on Earth and still considered a desert. There were no permanent residents. The research facility was in an old whaling building on Deception Island. There were glaciers, an active volcano, chinstrap penguins, and fossilized plants. The tests conducted were inconclusive, therefore not considered successful.

Quick's next journey would take him to the Gobi Desert in Mongolia to continue his study of the ancestors of the giraffe. He'd been there before and had many friends, Mongols, Uyghurs, and Kazakhs. Quick believed that the Aepycamelus or giraffe camel of the Gobi was the ancestor he sought, but he required scientific proof. The theory that the giraffe came from the Brachiosaurus didn't seem realistic to him. He'd left his Learjet 45XR complete with a working laboratory in Melbourne. Through inventions and patents, Quick had made his first million by age, 25. Now he bought land and real estate all over the world and pretty much did as he pleased. He gave most of his wealth to the needy, except what he kept for scientific research.

In Australia he had a message from NASA, they had a new discovery. With the Keplar Space Telescope they discovered an Earth-like planet: Keplar 452-b. It revolved around a sun much like ours. NASA wanted Quick to report to the Lyndon B. Johnson Space Center in Houston, Texas as soon as possible. Quick notified his crew and they were soon on their way. Quick communicated with NASA in flight, the International Space Center was now fully manned with six crew members from Japan, Russia, and the United States. The success of this mission made the moon mission more viable and important. The moon launch was now being moved forward due to the Keplar 452-b discovery.

The settlement was planned for one of three place: the Imbrium, Nectaris, or Serenitatis basins. That would be determined upon a closer inspection of the moon's surface.

On Quick's last visit to the Johnson Space Center, he and a team of experts designed the geodesic dome for six months habitation on the moon. It would be an icosahedron designed lattice shell on the surface of a sphere. Dr. Quick suggested they use a Buckminster Fuller design of continuous tension and discontinuous compression. With hardly any modifications two of the six space ships could be cannibalized into the material necessary for the construction of the dome. The remaining four ships could be fitted to carry the extra twelve crew members back to Earth once the mission was completed. Some Washington politicians didn't want to fund exploration or the possibility that a space colony could be established on the moon. Others wanted to send unmanned space craft to Pluto and Mars, which would do nothing to alleviate over population. NASA Headquarters in Washington, D.C. had leaked it to the press that they had received two donated telescopes that were superior in every way to the Hubble Space Telescope and they were being kept in storage. Quick suggested they take them both to the moon and place them temporarily or permanently to investigate and research the galaxy.

Blast off was scheduled from Japan, Russia, China, the United States, England, and France. The 36 astronauts chosen were highly educated in diverse scientific ways. Dr. Quick was chosen second in command of the Americans. Just before the launch Quick heard that his science fiction adventure manuscript was being made into a big budget movie.

The six moon landings were all perfect touch downs. The Americans and Japanese moved in with the Russians and French. They lived in the four space craft remaining until the dome was finished. Living in the dome was a luxury compared to space craft life. Once Quick got situated, he set up the two telescopes they'd brought along. While anchoring the base of the telescope, he found some unusual rock formations. He carried them back to the dome, upon further examination, he knew they were fossilized giraffe bones. Quick had been seeking these fossils all over Earth and now to find them on the moon was a most shocking discovery. He thought about his dream and about the script he'd written that was now going to be a movie.

The alien giraffes, Glorft and Guzal looked down at the moon dome from their invisible cloaked space ship. They spoke to each other telepathically. "Should we let our human-looking son, Qetazq know for sure about us?" "I think not, he could probably handle it especially since you've been sending him dreams, but the rest of Earth is not ready for our advanced technology and intelligence."

Coozeman

> *"There ain't no jackoff compared to that wonder-hole."*
> --Charles Bukowski

Quick never thought he'd be selling wigs to soul sisters, but life throws lots knuckle balls and rocks. The Korean folks he worked for were good people, but didn't have the gift for gab, plus they loved to eat garlic. Their breath could make your eyes water and skid stains in your undies. After the lady dropped a 45 on the floor on Quick's second day of work, he kept his eyes wide open. She came back awhile later and bought a wig and an extension from Quick, it happened to be the day he started getting paid on commission. It was a nice score, the lady asked him if he needed a piece. Quick said always, she meant her semi-automatic. Quick said he'd take both. He waited until the Koreans went to lunch and took her in the backroom and ravaged her. Quick ate that pussy then fucked her like Big Leroy breaking in a punk in Alcatraz. There was no tomorrow, yesterday, or future, only a sex machine gone haywire. That black woman screamed, "Bloody fucking murder, fire, rape, son of a bitch, you're the devil, you white motherfucker. The way you do sex is a dirty sin." She gave him the 45 and left before his bosses got back, She came back a week later with a friend, they asked Quick about some hair and a piece. "What do you have in mind ladies?" "Can you handle us both? We have a 357 magnum and a 9 millimeter." "Let's get a room nearby." They climbed into their Lincoln and cruised to liquor store for some libations. On the television was a fat chick telling Dr. Phil she'd lost one hundred pounds in one week. He told her she must've been cutting off body parts. Things got funky freaky real fast. After a couple of hours they were both sauced and snoring. Quick wrapped his new shooting irons in a towel and got the plastic bag from the bathroom trashcan.

He stopped in a bar on the way home and saw a ferret chained to a pool table. He asked what they fed it, a lady said the poor thing only eats Captain Crunch cereal. Quick bought the ferret for twenty dollars, he had no idea what to do with it. Maybe he could teach it to eat snatch.

Oceans of Purple

The old neighborhood was nearly unrecognizable. Acapulco de Juarez was the happening place from the 50's to the 70's for many of the Hollywood movie stars. Quick found himself fishing the beaches of Guerrero and ending up looking for a job in Acapulco. His Spanish was flawless and his skin so darkened by the sun, he was taken for a Mexican. In the mercado he saw three well-dressed Chinese men, he asked them for work. They said they worked for the Duke and he might be looking for help. Quick went along with them to a huge mansion. Number One Chinaman was the boss over eight other Chinamen. He asked Quick if he spoke any languages besides Spanish, Quick said no. After testing his ability to drive, Quick advanced in trust quickly and cared for the Duke's horses better than the Chinamen. He was soon made the official driver and was found most reliable. When Quick wasn't with the horses or polishing the 1955 maroon Rolls-Royce Silver Cloud, he explored Acapulco. Diego Rivera had painted many murals there. Frank Sinatra had a hotel, Errol Flynn, Gary Cooper, and Red Skelton had mansions there. JFK and Jackie took their honeymoon there. The Duke lived in a hotel at first with a long bed, then Johnny Weissmuller took over his room. Number Two gave Quick instructions to go to the airport and pick up an important guest for the Duke. He waited with a sign for the American black man. Quick loaded his three heavy suitcases into the baggage compartment of the car. The black man asked, "You don't know who I am?" Quick just kept an even look on his face. "Float like a butterfly....does that ring a bell? Do you speakee de English you dumbass taco bender?" Quick just smiled and pulled away from the curb. He thought the Champ was a chump. When they got to the Duke's he wrestled the three bags up to the Champ's room. The Champ gave him a whole dollar. That night as the Champ and the Duke got ready to feast, the Nine had been hard at work preparing the food. Quick prepared a potion of dried cockroaches and rat manure all crumbled into a fine powder. He asked Number Six which bowl of soup was for the Champ. He stirred in the powder. The Chinamen asked, "What would the potion do? What will happen?" "He will dream he is a cockroach being eaten by a giant rat." "How long will these nightmares plague him?" "It depends on how evil he is and if his heart ever becomes good, maybe forever." Quick went to the docks where he'd met a beautiful lady, named Liz. Her eyes were bottomless oceans of purple. There was a Van Gogh painting in the main cabin. They cast off and sped north toward the land of the gringos.

Brain Cells to Burn

Quick was taking a break at his grandmother's and his pal Stan came over. Stan sat in her favorite chair and started huffing and snorting acrylic glue from a spray can with his face buried in a brown bag. He'd look up and glue would be hanging off his mouth, nose, and eyebrows. Before Quick knew it he started screaming, "Little green men are coming out of the can." Then he hurled the can through his granny's plate glass window. Quick called a glass installer and they got it fixed that night before granny came home. As Stan was leaving he started singing, "This is a cowboy song, a kick in the nuts, steal your woman, screw your dog, set your horse on fire, piss in the gas tank of your Ford pickup truck. It's Pancho Villa on peyote, its Kenny Rogers getting corn holed……it's not bad." Quick's grandmother sat down to watch Jeopardy and said that window sure is clean, Quick told her he washed it. She knew something was cooking. A week later Stan got his car stuck in a sand dune at a keg party at Running Water Draw. He'd been drinking Everclear with grape Kool-Aid, Quick and some amigos hooked up a chain and were towing his car. Stan started punching it saying it was a giant ribbon snake, the chain snapped and knocked out his eyeball. He still made straight A's with one eye and without cracking a book or studying.

Apache Dream Lady

Quick had lots of stories about women he'd been with. Many were odd, but this one blew my mind. He told me he'd met Antelope Dancer at a powwow in Gallup. Her beauty took his breath away, it made his legs grow weak, she was indescribable. It was lust at first sight for both of them. They shacked up in a motel on Route 66 for a week, then traveled south along the Gila River camping until they hit Geronimo's raiding grounds. Antelope Dancer said she was a relative of Geronimo from the Bedonkohe Chiricahua Apache and Quick told her he was related to Wilma Mankiller of the Panther Clan of the Cherokee. They settled at a hot springs where the Apaches would rest after raiding into Mexico. It was surrounded by peyote cacti and datura. Dancer made a potion for Quick and her to shapeshift and to dream and seek visions. It contained Lophophora williamsii peyote, moonflower jimsonweed datura, yerba buena, yucca flowers, and mesquite beans made into pinole. Quick dreamed of a warrior sitting atop Mount Rushmore first offering sage to the four directions and chanting. The warrior moved over to sit on each president and he filled his long ceremonial pipe as he smoked, his body became enveloped in a turquoise cloud. He chanted four times and the mountain carvings crumbled into sand. The warrior did this to all four presidents until they disappeared. Then a huge cloud formed over the clean mountain in it was a herd of buffalo with mounted warriors chasing them. He ran and vaulted bareback onto spotted horse and they galloped toward the horizon. Quick woke up hearing the sounds of hooves running like thunder in the sky. In the sand were perfect images of George Washington, Thomas Jefferson, Theodore Roosevelt, and Abraham Lincoln. He was alone except for a tarantula, a scorpion, and a rattlesnake, looking at him, like he better hit the road.

Green around the Gills

Bukowski said you should always use lots of toilet paper when wiping your ass, because no one wants to smell your shit. Danny Quick agreed. He figured as you age more and more doctors want to explore your ass with fingers and snake wires with cameras up the old poop chute. A fucking man can't even die in peace without some racket making the rich richer, selling that game of prolonging life and escaping the inevitable. Quick had good insurance and a fine looking lady doctor, probing his nether region, so he thought it could always be worse. She found a hemorrhoid and wanted to burn it off with liquid nitrogen. He remembered a wart she burned from his finger that felt like a blowtorch melting his skin for a week. Danny thought folks might think he was a pussy, but he said forget it. His doc sent him to a proctologist, just a fancy name for an asshole specialist. The proc doc didn't look old enough to shave. He had two young ladies with him and he was supposedly teaching them about assholes and the torture thereof. They were sitting in three chairs giggling and having a good old time, it seemed at Quick's expense. He went behind a screen and disrobed and put on a backwards gown. The doc had him bend over and crack a smile. He listened to them snapping on their rubber gloves and the squishing sound of them lubricating their hands. Quick felt a finger worm up his rectum, soon joined by an entire fist, while the two ladies spread his cheeks even wider. He was squirming like a bloody zombie over a hungry shark tank. His guts started growling like a werewolf eating some screaming sheep. Deadly putrid farts started filling the air. The three docs were about to drop for a ten count. If you remember Linda Blair's projectile vomiting in The Exorcist that was Quick's asshole only it was diarrhea slimy shit. The two women started puking. The doc handed Danny one tissue to clean his ass of lube and shit and ran from the room. The women ran after him. Quick used the entire box of paper trying to clean up, it wasn't enough. He grabbed the blue beret and hounds tooth suit jacket of the proc doc, threw them on the floor and scooted around like a dog until his ass was semi-clean. The trio came back in the examining room just as Quick was ready to book. They all appeared a little pale and green around the gills. He smiled as they looked at him in horror.

Lady Death

Wearing straw sombreros, the tamale vendors set forth upon the city, like tarantulas on hot asphalt. Each had an area to cover and knew the best times to be there. They knew the big tippers and cheap skates, the putas, the drunks, the macho men getting some on the sly, and the chicken shit cowards. The aromas of chiles and garlic roasting over an open fire, then stuck in plastic bags to sweat and be peeled later. To be added to the spit turned tender goat, spooned into the masa smeared corn husks and steamed. Every morning to awake to these scents was a mouth-watering heaven. The vendors waited with their clean silver glistening pushcarts for the tamales, drinking coffee con leche. Bragging of their sexual prowess, numerous women and their attributes, boxing skills, old knife scars, ancestry, and general bullshit. Each cart was named for one of the thirty three states in Mexico. Selling tamales beat the hell out of factory or farm work.
La Familia squeezed its tentacles under every door and around the throats of all Latino business. There was no escape, no corner to hide in. The Mafia and Tongs were pussies in comparison. La Familia knew who snored and farted, who screwed whom, when people went to the toilet, and when a cockroach stole a crumb. Remaining in the shadows was impossible. A person had to eat, drink, breathe, and function. They caught Quick up when he was fifteen, no, that's incorrect. They'd never been separate, since Quick took a fall and kept his mouth shut, they knew Quick was a stand-up guy. The second bust for two kilos of smoke scared him into running. Denver was six bullets in the bull's eye of his life. Quick dug Larimer Square, Colfax, and Look Out Mountain, with all the white wooden crosses; where people had launched their cars off of cliffs into the arms of Lady Death. Quick must have been like a weed growing up through the concrete in a sidewalk for the law. It took the Feds setting

him up to put the steel bracelets on his wrists. They dragged him back to New Mexico. Luckily Vietnam was still happening and they needed cannon fodder, so Quick paid five thousand dollars to get an invitation to meet Victor Charles. Tricky Dick played Old St. Nick and stopped the war, so he went to Germany. The Russian red bear had them outnumbered twelve to one, but they could put a nuclear silver bullet in their heart any old time, what a Cold War fucking joke. Quick hung out in Crazy Sexy and Shit Park, the biggest whorehouse and hashish market in Europe, near Frankfurt's bahnhof. Amassing a small fortune in the black market, it was soon time to return to "the world". The law was waiting on Quick, smiling the smile of, now I'm-going-to-make-you-my-bitch. There were two choices, besides slim and none, fuck or be fucked. He chose the former. Quick's life was worth less than the piece of paper he wrote this on, but he was not afraid. He refused to be.

Cambodia

Hello Mr. Quickie,

Please understand me deeply. My name is Sabeen Adad from Syria. I am 63 years old christian woman, I am the CEO of SABEEN SEAFOOD LTD in Cambodia and Vietnam. I was in Syria when the islamist militant took over the state I live. The fights took my family lives and left me in a paralyzed condition. I am now trapped in the Hospital. I am not sure if I will live long. Raqqa is the region I live in Syria and is now controlled by ISIS militant. It is a horrible life here. I am secretly sending you this email in regards of my funds in Cambodia to be use for charity plans and humanitarian aid for the less privileged, the widows in your country. I can't go back to Cambodia anymore. The money there is $10,160.000.00. 20% should be for your commitment if you are interested. You will have to contact my lawyer in Cambodia.

Sabeen

Hello Sabeen,

I'm a 62 year old nasty motherfucker. I don't give a dog's turd about money. Send me photos of you naked, masturbating with a banana. Maybe you could send me some used panties from your smelly pussy, so I can jack off while dreaming of Cambodia.

Send some shrimp too,

Yours truly,
The Quick Dog

The Bricklayer

My dad, Quick was a master bricklayer. We built a huge stone fireplace for this rich rancher in West Texas. When we got all finished he tried to stiff my dad for payment. So my dad went up on the roof and did something. A few weeks later, the dude built his first fire, his house filled with smoke and did lots of damage. The rancher peered up the chimney to see if it was blocked, he thought it was all clear. He called my dad to fix it, my dad said have the money owed him in cash. The rancher had the money, my dad stomped through his dog area smearing his shoes, and then he went in and got his money, screwing up the rancher's new cream colored thick carpet. He got a ladder and went back on the roof and removed the piece of glass he'd put over the chimney. Dad threw piece of glass into the rancher's driveway, breaking it all to hell. We hit the road. After a few minutes, I asked my dad to remove his cowboy boots and put them in the back of the pickup.

The Jig

A few years before he'd put in a native stone hearth and stone corner reflector for a pot belly stove. The beautiful Mexican lady with the sad eyes was grateful. She made the best chicken enchiladas Quick had ever eaten. Her name was Magdalena and she grew garlic and raised goats for the market in Taos. Quick had learned stone work from his father. Magdalena had two nephews from Mexico, helping her on her little farm. She had told Quick that she'd like to rebuild an adobe chicken house and add onto her house. If he was ever in the region and had time to stop. He parked his sun bleached Ford under a cottonwood tree and made a tent and campfire. Quick and the boys built wooden forms to fill will caliche red clay and hay for the adobe blocks. After a few days the boys were able to make the blocks on their own. Quick took his stone hammer and Rose trowel and started laying the ground work for wall foundations. He dug down into a corner and hit a metallic sound. Prying the object loose, he cleaned it a bit and saw it was a Prince Albert tobacco can. He shook it and it rattled loud. Opening the lid, it was full of gold nuggets. Quick poured some out into his hand and knew it was a fortune. He yelled for Magdalena and the boys. When they arrived all breathless, Quick showed them his find. Magdalena almost fainted, the boys just grinned in awe. He scooped them all back into the can and gave them to Magdalena. The next day they went to the mining office and bank. She bought all three men new cowboy boots and hats and herself a dress. They pit barbequed a goat and danced a jig. Quick finished her addition and left, he had a rodeo in Gallup and a motel to build there

Cooking Dead Stuff

Quick's gal pal thought she was quite the chef. Always watching cooking shows and reading books and recipes. One day she was over spicing the food as usual. Quick said, "I think you used too much tarragon." Antoinette said, "You wouldn't know tarragon from a rat turd." He thought she did have a valid point, but she still went overboard. "Do you know how to shingle a banana cream pie?" "Well no." "Martha said to slice the banana at an angle and place them on the cream like a roofer would overlap shingles on a house." "She also said humans peel bananas from the stem end, while monkeys peel from the opposite end, which is much easier." Quick had lots of smart ass replies, but he kept his pie hole shut. One Thanksgiving he had to work, while Antoinette prepared the bird. When he got home the house was filled with black smoke, she had cayenne pepper, thyme, nutmeg, chives, cornbread, celery, chopped liver all over the cabinets, on the floor, even some on the walls. The stove was burnt all to hell. The turkey was just a small pile of black gray bones. Antoinette's mother and father had just arrived. Quick took them all to Taco Bell. They agreed to try again in two weeks. Antoinette had her French cook book from Mapie, the Countess de Toulouse-Lautrec, wife of the famous painter. Quick went bowling, when he returned, their house smelled terrible. Her parents were there, she had a spices everywhere. The meat was dripping green gravy and blood. Quick thought he might save it by putting it on the grill outside. When he got a close up whiff, he almost fainted. Quick asked Antoinette what kind of meat it was. She said, "Horse." He whinnied and started galloping around the house and right out the front door.

Gringo Tacos

Quick told me about the time he was persuaded to enter a jalapeno eating contest at the New Mexico State Fair. Before he could continue his story, he had an uneven grin on his face and he sort of wiped invisible sweat off his brow. He said he swallowed fifty one peppers mostly without chewing. Quick said this little Mexican woman that won, ate eighty seven. She got the trophy, the hundred dollars, and ate one more pepper, just for the hell of it. Quick said, "That night my stomach felt like an earthquake and a volcano were having a fist fight. The next day all those pepper seeds started flowing from me like molten lava." He stuck ice cubes his ass to no avail. Finally he spotted a can of Solarcaine in the bathroom closet. He sprayed half a can up his rump. It worked like magic, cooling his butthole down in relief. I told Quick about an adventure I had in Mexico and getting rolled for my wallet. I walked south of Juarez, looking for work. I saw a farm of hot peppers. They were growing, arbol, ancho, guajillo, chipotle, cayenne, and piquin. They gave me a bag to fill and told me I'd be paid twenty pesos a day. I worked until lunch time and they built a little fire and warmed beans, tortillas, and some goat. The food was delicious. After drinking a lot of water, I had to relieve myself. They pointed behind a cottonwood tree. All the workers seemed to be smiling. When I touched myself, it felt like someone had taken a blowtorch to my crotch. I yelled for help. One man came to my aid with a sack of salt and some tortillas. He motioned for me to rub the salt on my afflicted parts. I grabbed a tortilla and started masturbating like a sex crazed lunatic. All the Mexicans were laughing so hard in tears, I started laughing too and before I knew it the heat had stopped.

Blowing the Dog

Carol was Quick's first cousin. She was a real square and a holy roller. Sometime she'd drag her kids from door to door passing out religious pamphlets or go to the airport and preach loud with her bible. Quick grew up with her, so he tried to overlook her proclivities. At funerals and weddings there was no avoiding Carol and her brood, her husband reminded him of a quiet Nazi. Carol's sister, Gabby told Quick about her dog adventure. Carol had tried to breed French poodles, but after her third child she didn't want dogs in the house. She sold off all her pooches, except one, Pierre. The Nazi built the doggie an insulated dog house with thick plastic for a door flap. He spread hay for the dog to use as a potty area. One winter night, the temperature dropped down to negative thirty degrees. Carol's children and husband pleaded with her to let the dog inside, but she refused. That morning they found Pierre, damn near dead. His poor testicles were frozen solid. The Nazi put the dog on the kitchen table and started rubbing Pierre's balls. Carol blew warm air on his furry frozen nuts. Finally he thawed out and Carol said it was a miracle.

Spaghettio Capone

The farmer's market was filled with sounds of different people, languages, and accents selling their harvest. Hmong families with radishes, Bok choy, and long red curling Thai peppers. Amish ladies with white bonnets and men with shovel shaped beards and round hats selling jellies, cheese, and wooden toys. Germans with organic eggs, chickens, and beef. Polish with kielbasa sausage and czernina duck blood soup with prunes, cloves, and allspice. Old ladies with big straw sunhats and fans selling apples and peaches. Beekeepers with honey, comb, and candies. Children running and laughing. People haggling and filling their bags with fresh vegetables and fruit. Quick and I were people watching and listening to the sheer joy of being alive. He asked me if I was hungry and I said I could eat. On one side of the market all the food vendors were set up. The grills were sending up clouds of intoxicating odors. Most of the people were in line at a cart with an Italian sounding name. I told Quick they must know the best place to eat. It looked like five college kids were running the grill turning sausages and flipping burgers, one was placing the meat on buns, another was adding condiments, another was passing out sodas, another was working the cash register. The line was moving swiftly in a cloud of delicious sizzling meat. Quick was eyeballing this greasy haired Simon Legree that was yelling at the sweating workers. He had a pit bull on a chain and he would lift the dog off the ground, strangling it almost to death. I looked around for cops, I could see Quick gritting his teeth. We got to the cash register, Quick said, "Four bite dogs and two cokes." The order man looked at us like we'd just stepped off a Martian spaceship. "Four bite dogs, the ones you bite and they don't bite back, especially your asshole." The boss stepped forward, "Hey douchebag, did you call someone an asshole? Do you know who I am?" He pointed at a little sign on the cart that read Spaghettio Capone. Then he unleashed his dog, Quick had a way with animals. He petted it, spoke soothingly, and calmed it down. Before anyone could spit, he had Capone's nuts in a vise like grip. He put the leash around Capone's neck and tightened it until his tongue was hanging out and he was gasping for air. "Never be rude to your workers or hurt your dog. If you look mean at them or mistreat your animal, I'll return and I won't go so easy on you. Is that clear?" Spaghettio vomited and peed his pants. We left the market to much applause. Quick said, "Let's go amigo. I need to wash my hands."

The Most Beautiful Lady in Albuquerque

Bianca lived north of Albuquerque in the quaint little town of Corrales. She had a small adobe house with a wood burning stove and two fireplaces, Quick had built for her. She worked for a rich family, caring for their horses and tending their garden. They had chickens and an orchard of apple and plum trees. Her boyfriend, Buffalo played in a country and western band. Buffalo had moved from New York to New Mexico to avoid the fierce winters. He knew about plants and herbs. Buffalo was currently reading Stalking the Wild Asparagus by Euell Gibbons. He'd found an abundance of asparagus spears under almost every tree in the orchard. Steamed with butter, garlic, and peppers, the asparagus was delicious. Bianca shared the spears with the owners of the ranch, the Smithe's. They were usually only in New Mexico in the winters, being mostly snow birds from Boston.

Quick was Bianca's brother, he stayed most weekends with her and Buffalo. He worked for the Santa Fe National Forest Service as a surveyor for timber roads and a forest firefighter. Quick would leave Santa Fe every Monday to spend the week in the forests, staying in government quarters or in motels. He never rented an apartment, so he had a few ladies he stayed with or he'd head south to his sister's. Quick's main lady was a scientist in Los Alamos, she was a bit too serious for him. Her name was Brenda and she loved sex, but needed to be loosened up. Brenda was a brunette with a dynamite figure and a brain to match.

Quick spoke Spanish everyday on his job, he was the only Anglo. His crew was made up of five men including the crew chief. They would depart from Santa Fe in four wheel drive trucks and head north, unless there was a fire to be fought. The crew often saw an old lady in a sombrero carrying an easel and paint box. She would be out walking near Abiquiu or Ghost Ranch or Taos.

Quick asked about her, they said she was Georgia O'Keeffe, an old gringa painter.

Buffalo's band was playing at a honky tonk in Albuquerque, he asked Quick if he wanted to come hear them play. Bianca never went when he played because all the ladies loved his singing and usually wanted the whole enchilada. Quick never failed to make an acquaintance, when he turned on the charm. The Smithe's asked Quick to build them a patio with native stone and a barbeque pit, so he spent a few months coming every weekend to Corrales. There were many rich people that had haciendas and kept horses in the village.

John owned the biggest and most famous rock and roll club in Albuquerque. He was basically rolling in money. He liked the very best pot, liquor, and horses, plus he lived with a Playboy bunny. Toni was a centerfold and Playmate of the year. She was beautiful, lovely, perfect, and when she grinned at you, you were a gone motherfucking goose. Her hair was golden blonde, upstairs and down.

Quick happened to pass by John and Toni's bedroom while delivering weed and she was naked. She made no move to cover herself, she just laughed and smiled mischievously. Toni fell backwards onto the bed and let her legs fall apart revealing heaven on earth with a royal invitation. Quick was kind of frozen like a statue staring, he had a crowbar hard on. He knew right then he was going to tap that ass like a keg of Old Milwaukee.

John asked Bianca to ride his new horse, she asked if he'd been saddle broken. John said, the horse was gentle and tame. Bianca got on the horse and it reared and started galloping wildly away, John was almost shitting himself laughing. Quick jumped in his truck and chased down his sister on the unbroken horse. Quick wanted to stomp John face in, Bianca talked him out of it. John had lots of cop friends and low life amigos. Bianca had a good thing in Corrales. That's when Quick starting making his plans for revenge, he plotted and schemed and was diligent and patient. Quick spent a weekend with Brenda in Los Alamos. He explained what had happened to his sister. Brenda was reluctant at first to help Quick with his plan, but after some extra special love making, she agreed.

Toni started receiving flowers with poems of love. Quick asked her to come to Bianca's house to hear Buffalo's band practice. He taught her all the latest western dance steps. It wasn't long before he had her eating sugar cubes and apples from his hand like a fine filly. Soon Quick was making passionate love to Toni, while John was taking care of his bar. Finally one night Quick helped Toni pack her clothes and they drove north. They camped for a few days in the mountains, near a hot springs, it was a paradise of sheer bliss. Quick told her about his plan for her to stay with Brenda and take some college courses. Toni agreed if she liked Brenda and they got along. She was fed up with John being a tyrant and tired being a kept woman.

Brenda and Toni hit it off like long lost sisters. They traded off making love to Quick. He could've had them both together, but he preferred to concentrate on one lady at a time. Winter soon came, John had heard rumors that Quick had played back door man on him, making off with his woman. There was never any real proof of the cuckold. That came later, like having his fucking nose rubbed in horse shit.

The forests became impassible in winter, so Quick was laid off for four months of the year. Quick decided to visit some folks back east and take some turquoise jewelry to sell. Brenda and Toni drove him to the airport in Albuquerque. Quick felt like a king walking through the airport crowds with his two gorgeous ladies. Men rubbernecked with lust, women gawked with envy. There were reporters and cameramen there for the band Jethro Tull's arrival. They took photos of Quick, Toni, and Brenda. The ladies were all over Quick. Toni was recognized as a Playboy centerfold. The next day the headline in the Albuquerque Tribune read: The Most Beautiful Lady in Albuquerque.

The Asteroid

Quick was sitting in his lounger toking on some good ganja and drinking Black Cat Mosel wine. For some reason he had the television on golf, he thought it was a stupid game. He'd never played a game in his life, screw chasing a little white ball all over the place and getting skin cancer. He thought about scoring all those women and Tiger Wood's wife beating the hell out of his car with a golf club. Those dudes made some big bucks that was for damn sure. Quick started getting into the game and concentrating as he got higher and higher. He started talking to the golfers on the tube, he'd see a golfer take a swing and he would say, miss it by hair. Their ball would just miss the hole. He kept this up for a while, calling every golfer's shot. He let one guy make a hole in one, just to see if he wasn't hallucinating. Quick figured he had the kinetic power over golf balls. He had a ball go up and disappear in a flock of geese only to fall right next to the hole. Quick made balls fly into the crowd and knock toupees off bald fat men. He had several balls wedge between big chested women's ample boobs. He called his bookie and put in a bet on a long shot golfer to win. That day he made a bundle of loot.

He wasn't convinced that it was just him being high or what William S. Burroughs called letting your mind control objects around you in profound divine coincidence. Quick called in some bets on several basketball games and he remained straight. By sheer concentration he controlled the ball and the players, his winnings were beginning to draw notice from some unsavory characters. He took his lady Dani to Running Bare Nudist Colony for some recreation and relaxation. Quick worked on some writing projects for chapbooks from Texas and Belgium and Kolkata, India.

The radio announcers kept talking about the huge lottery prize about to reach a billion dollars. Crowds of people were lined up at all lottery ticket outlets. They all had their hard earned cash to invest in dreams of grandeur. The media kept saying the odds were near impossible for one single person to win the jackpot. Experts said you were more likely to get hit by an asteroid, than to score the bonanza.

Quick tried out his new control ability on several football games and Pick Four Lotto Games. He was in tune with the universe. He went and bought one ticket for the jackpot lottery. Quick stopped for fifty year old Scotch and the best hashish available. He took ten thousand dollars and Dani and he had a party. They got loaded and jumped up and down on the bed. Quick wiped her ass with hundreds and she wiped his with twenties.

That night when the winning numbers were called Quick did his magic mumbo jumbo. It worked like a charm. Dani and he went to sleep before going to claim their money. On the radio on the way to the lottery office, a soothing woman's voice came through the speaker saying how one individual had beaten the probabilities of chance. Dani and Quick were almost in the parking lot of the lottery office, when a dark object obscured the sun. The fiery molten asteroid instantly destroyed Quick's Oldsmobile, killing everyone within a half block radius.

Lucky for Quick and Dani, a block before, they'd stopped at a taco truck decided to get a snack and take a stroll and get some fresh air.

A Sea Of Mermaids

It all started the night Quick hurt his neck while trying to suck his own dick. This beautiful lady from East St. Louis, Missouri said, "I'm from the Show Me State, so fucking do it, if you want it done."

Half way to Jupiter fucked up, Quick seriously thought maybe his mouth would reach his pecker. She couldn't stop laughing when he told her to call an ambulance, because he was frozen in a human pretzel position. After Quick made up a lie about slipping on ice and the doctors and nurses looked at him and his hot sexy woman, like they were escapees from a porno film. Rosita, his little Missouri mule mockingbird, left him after he was admitted for an overnight stay. Quick shared the room with a fart bag, snoring, gagging, puking motherfucker, with his bed behind a thin curtain, just far enough away that he couldn't reach over and knock the shit out of him every once in a while.

Rosita, never being one to miss an adventure, went to an adult toy store while Quick was incapacitated. She told him later she went to buy a giant blue dildo and some edible panties for a treat for him when he got home. She left the jack off joint and got hit by a garbage truck with a snowplow blade mounted on the front. While the meat wagon came for her, a dude approached dressed as an evil clown. He was walking a pit bull and had a topless midget woman on his shoulders. The dog went wild when he saw Rosita's exposed ass and fine fluffy pussy bush lying in a snow bank. The clown threw the midget up in the air and tried to pull his monster animal off Rosita's butt cheek, but its teeth were clamped and locked.

A garbage man had no choice: he smacked the dog in the head

with a shovel, knocking it cold. The midget attacked the three man crew from the truck. The midget lady had the muscles of a weight lifter, she used to wrestle in Chi-town and Toledo. She started with a Damascus head-leg lock, used a chicken wing, went into a head scissors power bomb, took off her panties and ended with a Tree of Woe rubbing her itty bitty shaved cunt all over their faces, thoroughly whipping ass on all three men. The clown and the pint sized woman cradled Rosita and the dog until an ambulance arrived.

Quick was just getting out of the hospital, when Rosita was admitted. She had a double lawsuit going with a fast mouth attorney from television. It took some time to see any dough, but she hit the jackpot. They stayed together for a few months, until she got pissed and shit in his Boston Red Sox baseball cap and put it in the microwave with a fuck you letter. Quick figured she was more in love with that big blue dildo and that green paper than him.

He didn't give a fucking rat's ass. He'd always been a barracuda in a sea of mermaids.

Nevuary

Quick and the Pablo were burning rubber after a black Hummer full of Lizard's men. The Pablo was driving a souped up Ford 250 pickup in hot pursuit. The Hummer screeched to a stop, eight pretend Latino tough cholos unassed the vehicle. The fake crack house they intended to rip off was a front for a cash counting house of a black gang from Compton. Quick had his automatic machinegun with a mounted grenade launcher, plus some hardware that would turn that Hummer into a hot penny. Pablo had a bag of drones that carried high explosives, cameras of all type including infrared, tear gas, and concealment smoke. Four of Lizard's men took the front and two went around to the back. That left two men to be look outs and guard their getaway truck.

There was an elderly lady sitting on her porch next door with a nursing pregnant dog at her feet. Lizard's two men went over and grabbed the dog and kicked it to death. The old lady tried to stop them, but was pistol whipped for her effort. There were eight newborn puppies sniffing around their freshly dead mother. The men grabbed a pup and threw it into the air and blew it to pieces. They had thrown all the puppies, but one into the air and killed them, laughing hysterically. Pablo and Quick finally arrived. Quick hurled his razor sharp bayonet at the dude that held the dog, his arm was sliced off at the elbow. Pablo had the drop on both of them, but Quick wanted to make it up close and personal. He waded into both men, breaking bones and doing horrific damage. Finally he gave them both a pelvic punch, it pulverized their balls and they would never have sex again or urinate without agony.

"Every time you do that to someone, it even makes me hurt a little bit," Pablo said,

"I've heard a cockroach can live up to nine days with no head," replied Quick. "And some cats have nine lives."

They put their new dog in the pickup. Bullets were flying inside the house, but no one had come out yet. Pablo took the back and Quick hit the front, they brought in some heavy munitions. Pablo had Quick's six, he had two drones watching over him like guardian angels of death. Civilization dropped off Quick, like a snake shedding its skin. He was no longer human, he was a killing machine. Quick threw several shurikens, but most of his killing was close quarters combat. Blood, brains, viscera, eyeballs, mismatched limbs, and several heads and torsos littered the house. Stacks of money acted as sponges for the rivers of blood.

The party was soon all over, but the crying and Quick was all out of mercy. The two hombres he'd messed up would report back to Lizard.

"What do you want to name our dog?"

The little puppy was licking their faces as they split. "How about Snake?"

"We lost Snake in Afghanistan. Do you think this might be him reincarnated?"

"Hell yea. Snake, it is then."

Quick and Pablo were on a stake out on a stream. There had been reports of drug shipments and truck loads of Hispanics sold into slavery. It was a dangerous assignment, so they were chosen as hell on wheels.

Quick's eyes narrowed to slits, his nostrils dilated testing the air for danger. He disappeared into the chaparral, like a wild creature of the wind. The splashing might've been a grass carp or gar turning over in the water, but never leaving things to chance is how you remained alive. The tree frogs soon resumed their romantic croaking for a mate. Pablo slithered through the high grass downstream before rising. Quick jacked a clip of tracers into his automatic weapon. Pablo approached the fire stealthily, to warm his hands. Something was bothering him; Quick could see a smoldering anger, a bordering insecurity.

"What is it?" Quick whispered.

"Not sure."

A bullet tugged at his sleeve, burning a furrow up his arm. Another bullet blew the heel off his boot. An unearthly scream cackle echoed through the canyon. The heavy boom of Pablo's grenade launcher followed the muzzle flashes of the attackers. At a run, Quick fired bursts of M-16 tumblers. The canyon grew quiet.

They scouted the barranca, finding the tracks of two men. They rousted a diamondback, a covey of quail, and some sage hens. Pablo had some tesquino corn beer and jerky. They built up the fire and filled their bed rolls with stones. Taking the high ground, they drank and waited. The stars and clouds swam through the skies. The night was a brujo in disguise.

Quick spoke quietly to Pablo of a story he remembered from his mom that Soldier, his father had told her. She'd written it down for him to read when he might be able to understand about war.

A few stars hung overhead like nail holes in a black wall. Soldier looked up and continued walking at a brisk pace toward the barely discernable tracks. His part in the war was always following warily a few feet behind. He was once an elite shadow of a Long Range Reconnaissance Patrol. Chained dogs roamed in the yards of slumbering humanity, growling at the gates of hell. He needed to fight again, to kill to prove himself worthy. Some nights in the waning darkness, Soldier would recall the adrenalin abyss whisper rush, orgasmic sweat soaking his body. Uncontrollable dreams of clean kills and remorselessness stirred an inferno in his loins. Looking around, Soldier saw graveyard emptiness; his heart leaped green mountains of verdure. It had been over twenty five years since he last tasted the exhilaration of a human hunt. The evocation of his demons freed and condemned him at the same time. The tracks beckoned him. He carried his cross every time his eyelids closed, every step he took. Soldier crawled through the underbrush into a distant time. He was miles into Laos, behind enemy lines. Ahead dressed in tan, the uniform of an officer, his target leaned against a thick stand of bamboo, weapon out of reach. Soldier's knife came alive in his fist. He became a dervish of death. Four humans lay staring in carnage at the jungle canopy with lifeless eyes. The stench of blood filled his nostrils, his mouth stretched in an unholy smile. There was no memory of the three men. The woman officer was like a horror movie, he saw his right hand yank her head back, his left draw the blade in an arc across her soft throat. Her head dangled from a flap, death gurgled crimson onto the jungle floor. Her body slumped; her cap askew, long blue black hair blossomed free like a waterfall at midnight. Soldier stood over her and studied her face. Even death could not remove or erase her beauty. Dark almond eyes stared at him questioningly, accusingly, his tortured soul screamed, he knelt beside her. In a different world he might have been a young man proposing marriage. He raised her tiny exquisite hands to his lips, tears spilled a turmoil of hate and love. Soldier heard voices. "Hey mister, have you got a cigarette?" a girl asked. He looked in the direction of the voice, he was back. Two lovely ladies were looking at him inquisitively. Soldier offered them two of his smokes. They lit up, their lipstick bright on the filters. "Some men are after us, can you help us? We need a place to hide." He looked deep into their eyes and felt his bayonet in his pocket like an old scar.

"That's deep my brother." Pablo said. "I heard a tale about some folks we know. Nobody knows for sure if it's true. It's under the rug so to speak."

The U-Haul truck was parked in front of their building with five of Juanita's friends hauling out her furniture and clothes. Billy was sitting on the curb, crying with his pistol in his lap. Quick circled the block and parked a distance away, he wasn't letting any harm come to his little sister or her amigas. He found a brick in the alley and snuck up on Billy and tapped him behind the ear, just hard enough to make him unconscious. Quick took the pistol away from Billy and stuck it in the back of his belt. Juanita moved home again, she saw Billy on the campus, but he kept his distance. Billy had a terrible gambling problem, Texas Hold 'Em had apparently ruined his life. Quick thought first of his sister, but he had no ill wishes toward this young man. Juanita joked that she would run a credit check on her next boyfriend.

Quick remembered Juanita's first boyfriend, she'd tried to live with. Quick referred to him as the motherfucker. He was a pure evil mean rotten son of a bitch, but Juanita didn't see it that way. Since their parents died when a drunk had crossed the center line on the Pacific Coast Highway, they were the only family each other had. The motherfucker had a baby by a crack whore, he brought the under nourished kid home for Juanita to care for.

One night the motherfucker was blasted on PCP and he put the baby in the microwave oven and started it. Luckily Juanita saved the baby. Then he put her cat down the garbage disposal. The cat got its tail mangled and ground off. Juanita called Quick for help. He arrived wearing a red Santa Claus cap, he carried a chrome plated 357 and a sledgehammer. The motherfucker tried to run out the backdoor\, but the thrown hammer was a fraction faster than his legs. The five pounds of steel hit him with a sickening thud, fracturing his spinal column. Quick led his sister, the baby, and the cat to his car and started it to get the heater working.

Quick soon came out with a rolled up rug, tied in several places, he eased it into the trunk of his ride. Juanita asked, "When will that monster be back?" Quick said, "Maybe next Nevuary."

The Magic Rabbit

The poet was at the crucial point of a poem he had been slaving over for weeks when the phone rang.

"Hello, honey. Could you please pick up a loaf of bread and three small pumpkins? I don't want them too large. The big pumpkin's pulp is too stringy for pies. While you're at it, we could use a gallon of milk. Okay?"

"Yes, dear," Quick replied. When he hung up, he stared at the blank paper. His thoughts had been so disrupted, no words were there. He chewed on his pencil, giving himself a headache. He went and opened the refrigerator door, not knowing what he was doing. Looking under the refrigerator, he found one of the cat's half eaten toy mice. He tossed this from hand to hand. The words had vanished. Quick was sure the poem would have won him the Pushcart Prize. Well, he thought, I might as well go to the store. It was a pleasant day, the tulips were in bloom and the birds were chirping. He got in his car and was driving down the street when a rabbit darted in front of him. He swerved, but couldn't avoid the bunny. Getting out of the car, he noticed the rabbit wasn't dead.

The poet removed his jacket and wrapped it around the injured rabbit. He took it to an animal shelter, where it would be cared for. As he left, he was two blocks away when his tire went flat. Getting out the jack, spare tire, and lug wrench, he proceeded to change the tire. One lug nut was extremely tight; Quick busted a knuckle and saw stars of pain. Just as the blood started oozing from his hand, the words to the poem came to him, crystal clear. He hastily grabbed tissue to staunch the blood and started scribbling, before they escaped him again. When his wife got home, she asked him about the groceries. He just stared at her like she was a stranger.

Jail Roping

Twenty years driving through the devil grin moonlight, made Quick aware of the magic of darkness. He swerved to avoid a turquoise raccoon ambling across the road. Listening to Bob Dylan's: The Ballad of Pat Garrett and Billy the Kid, Zimmie honking hard on his harp. Mexican guitars and tambourines filled the air. Thoughts of his cat, Paloma that had recently died made his bifocals misty with tears. Quick lit a roach of Columbo and a seed popped and burnt his nuts causing him to crash into a tree. Quick woke up in jail, he'd been there before. He recalled a story about John Dillinger and his side kick, Homer Van Meter. Homer had taught himself how to rope flies with thread, while inside. Quick started unraveling his shirt, much to the amazement of his cellmate.

Zupidx

Dreaming of Robert Duvall, Blue Duck, and Lonesome Dove, then him telling me, "I love the smell of vagina in the morning," just as the helicopters swoop in with napalm, WHISKEY TANGO FOXTROT. Quick sent his money to zypidxygsrzmn4ck4tkax Male Member Enlargement $39.95 for a guaranteed four inches and a huge girth growth also. When the pills arrived Quick popped one and drove around, suddenly his penis escaped. It leaped from his pants and out the window and strangled ten seagulls and four Canadian geese, then squirmed down his pants leg coughing up feathers and almost killing Quick in a car/dog crash Later it jumped out and gorged down a statue of Henry "the Fonz" Winkler and spit it through a Frank Lloyd Wright house. Quick made a seriously bad move, b going over to see his band, Concrete Okra. They were working on a song called I Wanna Suck Yoko Ono's Left Titty, when Quick's wild Johnson gulped down the drums and bass guitar. Hearing the doorbell, a girl with squinty crusty eyes asked Quick for a donation for a political party, he handed her toilet paper to clean her eye boogers. She came inside and he told her of his dilemma, she applied situational ethics. That night his boa strangled her dead, Quick thought well since I'm going down I'll do some good. He took his slingshot to work and picked out some pebbles on the way. Inviting his cruel boss outside, Quick pointed up. When the little Hitler bastard boss, looked up, his mouth opened, Quick shot and snapped the longest icicle hanging down. The frozen spear knocked Adolf's teeth out and protruded from his anus. Quick figured he'd be locked up for a while. He guessed his dreams of an aardvark farm were out of the question now.

The North Pole Blues

My cousin married a coal mining hillbilly from West Virginia. His hick accent was thicker than chunky peanut butter. His brother, Quick could do a perfect English accent, he'd score chicks with it. Quick was a top shelf bullshit machine, I figured one day somebody would stick his nuts in a vise. He was always talking about Davy Crockett and wrestling bears. I'd thrown down with him a few times and he was a salty son of a bitch. When he'd try to put a hold on me, I'd open up a can of whoop ass, I trained for Vietnam in Ft. Polk, Louisiana. Also with a Puerto Rican guy that beat Bruce Lee in Madison Square Garden. Maybe Quick could handle a bear, but fighting to me was like knowing how to swim or ride a bike, it came natural. Out of the blue, Quick invited me to a concert at the North Pole. He said he'd won some free tickets with transportation included. The Reston, VA, based Molson Brewing Co. planned to send about 250 people for a four-day trip that included cruising the Arctic Sea from Resolute Bay aboard an icebreaker. The Red Hot Chili Peppers would entertain the group while aboard the icebreaker. A dude in the band named Flea raised sheer hell on bass guitar. The temperature was warm for the concert featuring Metallica, Hole, Moist, Cake, and Veruca Salt. We saw huge bears eating seals, Polar and Kodiak. The concert was in Tuktoyaktuk, a village on the Beaufort Sea. The winners along with about 400 townspeople gathered in a heated tent for the show. Quick and I partied with some funky ladies from Hole and some Eskimo babes. The stars were pulsing hypnotic blue diamonds. The wind was moaning on the tundra. Quick decided to wrestle a bear, I guess he just got tired of living. The Polar bear hit him once with his massive claws and his head went flying, the bear picked up his body and strolled away. I went over and looked at Quick's head, he was still smiling.

Chicken Foot Soup

The tall black guy was standing on the bench in the three sided shelter looking up Greenfield for the bus.

"I just got back from Atlanta and man it's hot down there," he said.

"Looks like you got a tan," I replied. His white pal started laughing.

"Every house down there has three bedrooms and three bathrooms. You don't have to share or put your ass where anybody else has."

"Did you see the Stone Mountains? Or any hillbillies eating peaches?" They both laughed as their bus arrived.

An older coffee colored lady had been sitting at the bus stop listening to our conversation. "Are you going to work?" she asked.

"No, afraid not."

"You lose your job?"

"Something like that," I replied.

"You're cute, you want to come home with me for some afternoon action?"

"Sorry, I better take a rain check. I don't have any condoms."

She opened her purse and pulled out an assortment. "I can give you the best blowjob you ever had. If you don't believe me, take off your boot."

Wondering what she had in mind, I obeyed. She started sucking and blowing on my big toe, like it was a tuba. About that time the cops drove up. I started hopping down the street, doing the chicken foot, waving my boot and sock in the air, a blue rubber stretched over my toe. I gazed back and the cops were laughing their asses off, while the grinning woman waved goodbye.

Making Love to the Rain

The gray black clouds full of dirt streaked tears and blood weep down onto yellow withered crops, as the farmers sob for their hungry families. They are forced to leave home, to find work and seek existence far away on freight trains. In smoke filled factories they build automobiles by day and work the stockyards by night. Saving, hoping, praying, and missing their loved ones.
Thinking about the war just fought and promises made for a better life in the land of the free and home of the brave. While years heap up like golden maple leaves in Quebec or snowflakes on a Tucumcari coyote moon night on Route 66. Sometimes the heart is nothing more than a clock measuring life, death, earth, moon, and sun. All moving in circles, like wise nomads, the square corners, box you in like prisoners not free buffalo and wild mustangs. My garden grows dark as I try to make love to the rain and all that is left is dirt streaked tears of dusty fading memories. The plants whisper with poetry. Orange Chinese-lanterns with voices of Li Po and Tu Fu, purple blue Concord grapes with voices of Dylan Thomas and Edgar Allan Poe, juicy blackberries with voices of Walt Whitman and Longfellow, green and red onions with voices of Bukowski and William S. Burroughs, plum and beefsteak tomatoes with voices of Ginsberg, Corso, and Kerouac, dwarf sour cherry tree with voices of Pablo Neruda and Octavio Paz.

It's Getting Hard as I Write

I can look at all the centerfolds and stroke the bone any way you want, but the jizmo refuses to cooperate, until I read or write about it. Or the real thing, of course always works wonders. I moved to Milwaukee from New Mexico and lived with my aunt and three cousins. They were all major prick teases. My aunt liked to sit naked at her dressing table and wait until I looked in, then she'd powder her beautiful tits and hairy pussy and smile, pretending she couldn't see me in her mirror. I wanted that woman so bad I could taste it. I closed my eyes and fucked her a thousand times.

Her youngest daughter would screw anything with a heartbeat. I caught her eating an amazing black chick's snatch and I made them both suck me and fuck me many times, until my weenie was ready for vacation. She used to open her cunt lips and play with herself and let me do anything I wanted. That was always a fun game.

Her sister was a redhead; she wore bikinis with her cunt hair sticking out. She used to let me put suntan lotion on her tits and finger fuck her, then she'd blow me into oblivion. I never got to tap that, she got religion first.

My third cousin was half Mohawk. I took her to Juarez, Mexico, with a cat named Reefer. I took her to a whorehouse, where I let her watch the matron check me for critters. She kissed my dick and fingered my asshole. My cousin got so hot, we split from Reefer and fucked each other's brains out. Her pussy was tight, but not educated. After a week with me, she graduated with honors.

Respect

The small town newspaper headline reads: Man defecates on father's grave. A source that wishes to remain anonymous reported to the police a suspicious man in the cemetery. The man was doing disgusting things. He had his trousers lowered and was making foul grunting and farting sounds, as he defecated all over a tombstone.

On closer examination, it was discovered that it was his very own father's grave.

The police arrived immediately and confronted the man. A slight struggle ensued with the inebriated man. Luckily, the cemetery was almost empty. They subdued the perpetrator and placed him in the rear of the police car.

"Damn, Sarge, did you ever see anybody shit like that? That stuff is sprayed and plastered like stucco on that granite tombstone."

"Hell, no, I've never seen anything like that. That shit is incredible, no telling what that crazy bastard has been eating and drinking. I've got shit smeared on my uniform. I've got a good mind to shoot the son of a bitch right here."

From the rear of the car: "You guys aren't going to waste me for that, are you?"

"What in the hell are you doing shitting in our graveyard?" the sergeant said.

"That's my so-called father in the grave," the perp said. "All of my life, I looked up to him and trusted him. He was a hard worker and always brought his check home to the family. He boozed it up sometimes, but I figured he earned it. My mother always bitched and nagged him, he was due a little escape. I cherished the man.

"A month after he died, my sisters came forward with the truth. He'd been sexually and mentally abusing them most of their lives. My older sister found out my father had started in on my two younger sisters and told the entire story to our mother.

She refused to believe a word of it," the perp said. "She had my sister put in a detention home, where she was sexually abused by guards and lesbians. She underwent shock treatments in a mental hospital, until she died very young. My younger sisters went through hypnosis and mental and drug therapy, until they also lost their minds and way.

"I never suspected a thing," the perp said. "If I had, I would have killed this fucker long ago. I've been drinking red box wine and eating diarrhea pills for a week. Now you know my story, if you want to take me to jail, I understand. At least you know where I'm coming from."

"Sarge, we can't arrest this guy," the patrolman said. "He only did what we would've done ourselves in the same situation."

"We had a complaint filed, but maybe we can smooth things over. If we let you go, what will you do?"

"I'm thinking about finding a shovel, digging the motherfucker up, then shoving the handle up his ass, getting some gas, and making him into a crispy critter."

"Look asshole, you're lucky we're letting you go. Don't press your luck." They pulled in front of the bus station. The sergeant said, "Now don't come back until after I retire and that's in five years."

"Thanks, officers."

The bus pulled out.

The patrolman grinned at the sergeant. "Wipe that smile off your pie hole. You're cleaning the stench out of this car, while I change uniforms and get a maple glazed doughnut."

Maria Takes a Powder

A television set showing clips from an old Cheech and Chong movie, before the play starts to set the mood.

Jimi Hendrix music from Axis Bold as Love, then toned down as the play starts.

Fake weed smoking with electronic cigarettes. Some fights and maybe gun play or knives and fake blood.

Characters:

Maria, Joe Snow, Little Joey, Fatty, and Nasty Jack

Set:
A room with a door and peephole, 2 kilos of flour, a washing machine (fake or real), fake guns and fake knives. (optional Electronic cigarettes to look like joints)

Off Stage: People to bang on door and buy dope
Little Joey could be played by a doll (if no kids are available)

Before the curtain opens a television starts playing a Cheech and Chong movie with people laughing like crazy behind the curtain. Raise the curtain slowly, the television soundtrack goes silent, but the picture stays on partially facing the audience. Jimi Hendrix starts playing a solo and Nasty Jack start shredding his air guitar. Fatty is sitting in a chair close to the front door. There is a loud banging and Fatty takes a look out the peep hole of the reinforced steel door. He is cradling a combat shotgun.

Fatty

Yo, Boss you better come take a look at this.

Jimi Hendrix music was bouncing off the walls, Joe Snow turns the volume down. He steps up to see what has Fatty's attention, Fatty is usually able to handle any situations that arise with his sawed off shotgun if need be.

Joe Snow

Who the hell is that? I wonder what she wants.

Fatty

She looks harmless, Boss. I don't think she's a narc.

Joe Snow

Well I'm glad you cleared up that big mystery. Get your skinny ass over in the corner and cover me with that scattergun, just in case it's a take down. Nasty if you turn that music up again, I'm going to shove your air guitar right up your ass.

Nasty Jack

Okay Boss, you're the Boss.

Joe Snow scowled at him. Fatty just laughed. They opened the door to the pleasant looking Latina lady. The young woman stood on the steps, with a colorful shawl draped around her shoulders. She rang the doorbell and tapped her sandaled toe impatiently. Nasty Jack was already snoring like a constipated chainsaw. Joe Snow opened the door.

Joe Snow

Yes, may I help you?

Maria

Busco trabajo, quiero ser la nana?

Fatty

Wait a minute, Boss, she no speakee de English.

Joe Snow

Back off, Fatso. My Spanish is little rusty, but I think she's looking for work and she's a babysitter.

Maria

Cuanto ninos tiene?

Joe Snow

She wants to know how many kids we have. Someone must've told her we need a babysitter. I hope they didn't tell her our last one died of an O.D.

Fatty

Boss man, we need her bad. I'm tired of all those stinky shitty diapers. Little Joey is a crawling poop machine, don't take any offense. He almost got his little hands in the product last time we were cutting and weighing it.

Joe Snow

Yea, I know what you mean. If I ever catch his two timing mama, it's going to be cement shoes for that witch. Senorita, habla English?

Maria

A leetle.
She made a small space between her thumb and index finger.

Joe Snow
Como se llama?

Maria

My name ees, Maria Consuelo Theresa Jesusa Chavez y Baca.

Fatty

Whhooeee, what a name.
Fatty whistled. Joey elbowed him in the ribs.

Joe Snow

We have un muchacho, mi hijo, Little Joey.

She smiled and walked past them, looking at Nasty Jack in dismay. Joe Snow led her to his son's room.

Maria

Madre de Dios, aieee Chihuahua.

Making the sign of the cross several times fervently. Before getting the toddler, bathing him, and beginning the cleaning. Maria washed mountains of diapers, dirty clothes, dishes and scrubbed floor and walls. She was like a whirlwind of cleanliness. She had Fatty and Jack (he wasn't nasty anymore) jumping to her commands. Sometimes when they didn't understand her orders, she would mime what needed to be done. Little Joey loved Maria. His favorite game was to play with his little penis, while she sang Cuban love songs.

Joe Snow, Fatty and Jack made money hand over fist selling their near pure cocaine, fresh from South America. They received many customers, especially in the middle of the night. Maria was not pleased, she complained and complained to no avail. One morning, after a particularly busy night, the three men were sleeping late. Maria removed all the bullets and shells from their revolvers, machine guns and shotguns. She gathered up all the money, which she stopped counting after $379,000 and packed it in a suitcase with Little Joey's clothes. Taking the bricks of uncut cocaine, she slashed them open and dumped them in the washing machine and started the heavy duty cycle. She wrote a short note-her English had improved some. "White powder ees no bueno for Little Joey. Too much noise at night, with your putas, mota and whiskey. I take heem home with me to Havana. Adios pendejos." Maria cradled Little Joey in one arm and carried their suitcase in the other. The sun was shining like a zillion diamonds swimming in a lake of blood. Little Joey carried a tiny yellow rubber chicken and was all smiles. They settled into their airplane seats bound for Veracruz, with connections to Cuba. Maria ordered rum and cola and a double milk. Joey squeezed his chicken, it made a peep.

Baked Alaska

The first time I saw Jeffrey Dahmer, was while reading on South Second in Milwaukee, Wisconsin at an art gallery parking lot right across from the Club 219 Bar and the Ball Club. Dahmer picked up many of his victims in that neighborhood of gay bars and taverns by drugging them and dragging them home. After murdering them, he would saw and slice them up and freeze the portions he wanted to eat. He tried to dissolve the remainder of their bodies in his apartment in a barrel of chemicals without much success. His neighbors all complained of terrible smells, stench, and bizarre sounds. He worked at the Ambrosia Chocolate Factory nearby, later everyone wondered if he'd put human flesh in their candy.

At the poetry and music event, this zany guy with a long hillbilly beard wearing a funky sun dress was the announcer. He had a briefcase full of two dollar bills with cut up newspaper inside to make them look like lots of money. After each poet read or musician performed he would give them a bundle of cash. At that time I was reading with a bass player and we were really raising hell, it was outside, so all these gay guys came from the surrounding bars, a guy jumps on stage and starts playing harmonica. Later I discovered he was, Jon Paris, from the Johnny Winter Band. I saw Jon's band a few years later at B.B. King's Club in Times Square. We were really cooking and we did a few more poems. I grabbed the entire brief case of money and threw it up in the air, it was a riot, sort like if all the monkeys in the zoo took peyote and escaped. There was squealing and screaming and elbows all over eighteen dollars at most. The handsome well-dressed blonde man with a hypnotic stare just stood there with his arms crossed unfazed. He watched the melee for a while then walked away like he was disgusted.
A few months later, I was reading at the Hotel Wisconsin. The

place was the epitome of old world charm, chartreuse marble floors, French art deco, and bronze with a carved walnut main desk. The bar area where the readings took place had maroon blood red carpeting and multicolored lava lamps on each table. It was dark and smoky and full of lounge lizards. Everyone seemed to be on the make, it had almost a circus like orgy atmosphere. I was working with a black sax player named Big Frank, he could blow like an elephant or make the small hairs on the back of your neck stand up and dance. When he played Take Five by Dave Brubeck, it was his signal for trouble. We were doing gigs at a lot of liquor stores on the rough north side of town. We had to beware of drunks and stickup dudes. I saw this blonde man with a thousand yard stare, he seemed familiar, but I couldn't place him for certain. Frank started playing our trouble song. I looked all around and saw who Frank was nodding at. We soon ended our set and went to collect our chump change fee. Frank packed up his horn as I set out some books to sell. Jeffrey Dahmer bought three of my chapbooks, then offered to buy me a drink, and wanted to chat. I'm glad I wasn't too thirsty and I had a few people waiting to buy books. Several weeks later Big Frank calls me to look at the television and there was Dahmer being dragged to jail in chains. I took Frank out for steak and lobster and Baked Alaska.

The cops came by my house after Dahmer was in jail. They asked me about my chapbooks and if I was friends with Dahmer. I said hell no, check my freezer if you want. That was good enough for them.

The next day, Charles Plymell stopped by for an overnight visit. He was on his way to Kansas to visit William S. Burroughs and Ginsberg

Black Knife

The raptor stood and sniffed the air, catching the scent of human. Roaring from the thick brush where it had been foraging for grubs, it tried to sink its claws into Jik. The raptor was almost ready for winter hibernation or Jik wouldn't have been fast enough to step inside the grasping raptor's reach and stab it repeatedly in the heart. His knife gleaming blood red in the sun was long and razor sharp, deflecting rib bone, fat, and muscle. He ensured that it was dead, and found two old bullet holes that could account for the hatred and lack of fear in the fierce raptor. Jik sang over its body, praising its bravery. Caw flew down as Jik began skinning the raptor. The raven went in search of Black Knife and Dancing Fox. They accompanied it to the carcass of the raptor, helping with the skinning and fletching. Wrapping the best cuts of meat for the tribe, they built a travois to drag behind their palominos. They watched out for their enemies, the Tlazolteot, who would sacrifice and eat them before considering the raptor. They were called filth eaters and preferred human meat over animal. The Tlazolteot were said to be in league with the devil; they had traded their souls to become shaman and shape shifters. Black Knife was Dancing Fox's father, he was a powerful healer and he was teaching her about herbs. Dancing Fox's skill was near surpassing her father's. They had found Jik near death from full body wounds, but his head was the biggest problem. His memory of where he came from was a mystery. The elders in the village could not make sense from Jik's mutterings while he was feverish. He spoke in many languages, Apcuitl, Navctl, Athabascol, and their enemy the Tlazolteot. His strength came back slowly over time, but he remained a mystery in many regards. The maidens of the Apcuitl went out of their way to see or help Jik. He was a handsome man, strong, and quick with a smile or joke. The children loved him. Leaping Moon seemed the only warrior to distrust and not like him. People thought it was jealousy over how close Jik had become with Dancing Fox. "The raptor almost took your head off, Jik. Your wounds have not had time to heal; you are not ready to hunt." Black Knife said. As they stopped to rest their horses, Dancing Fox gathered rose hips and mullein. Black Knife watched his daughter with approval. "I can't remain in camp forever. My memory may never return, but my strength has. The raptor meat will feed the people for a week, its death was meant to happen." Against this logic, there could be no argument. Caw flew down from its scouting flight and perched on Jik's shoulder. He seemed to speak to the bird and the bird chirped and bobbed in answer. "We mustn't be caught out in the sandy flats. We will soon have company," he warned. Grabbing what he could of the meat; Jik cut loose the drag poles. "There's no time for that, let's ride," he exclaimed. Riding down out of the hills of mesquite and sage, the horses picked their way through the rocks. Swirling clouds enveloped the edge of the desert, something was heading their way swiftly. Jik pushed Black Knife and Dancing Fox up the trail; he turned and drew a silver metal rod from his tunic. Dragging it along the ground it made a burning smell and the sand wiggled and writhed, coming alive with energy. They kept going at a tiring pace for the horses. At least twenty Tlazolteot warriors were riding like there was no tomorrow. They were killing their horses; flecks of hot white foam soaked the poor beasts. As they hit the sand, it became alive, shadow demons and dusty monsters pulled horse and rider into early graves. The vegetation turned black and the sky into a fiery sheet of flickering hues. Hideous screams echoed through the land. Three men were all that remained of their raiding party. Enough to carry the tale back to their tribe of blood thirsty cannibals. Pig Tooth, leader of the Tlazolteot would never stop until Black Knife's tribe the Apcuitl were wiped from the face of the earth. After he heard the story of the living quicksand, he would know he was not the only powerful magician. Black Knife rode on ahead, leaving Jik and Dancing Fox as a rear guard. Knowing Jik would protect his daughter and his abilities were far beyond any warrior. They pulled together a brush shelter to diffuse their fire, after first caring for their horses. To be on foot in this hard country could be the difference between a long and short life. Dancing Fox put some raptor meat on to cook while Jik gathered wood for the coming night.

As the sun lowered in the sky the temperatures fell off swiftly. Dancing Fox was sore from riding a long distance at a break neck pace. "Lie down and try to relax," Jik told her after they had eaten. Caw floated down with several owls to keep watch over the camp. Jik laid out several scraps of meat for all his feathered friends. He knew they would warn him of any unwanted guests. He slept sitting up facing away from the fire so it wouldn't interfere with his night vision. Their remaining trip back to the tribe was uneventful. Black Knife's tracks were visible on the trail. Tall green blue trees rose out of the valley mist. In the forest flowers and silence watched the butterflies dance upon the wind. Juan Two Raptors and Leaping Moon were having a heated argument about a war party. Leaping Moon wanted to gather the warriors and travel south across dangerous territory in hot pursuit of the Tlazolteot. His plan would leave the village unprotected and open to attack from other enemies. Juan Two Raptors, Dancing Fox's cousin, warned against rushing off without a council of the elders. There were some for war and some for peace; this seemed like a time for more rational thought, Black Knife and Jik agreed. Jik, not being of the tribe had no say, which Leaping Moon was quick to point out. "Jik has fought alongside the Apcuitl like a brother. I say we adopt him into our tribe," Juan Two Raptors said. "We don't know where he came from. He has the unknown powers of a shaman. He speaks the language of our enemy. I say he is a spy and we should kill him," exclaimed Leaping Moon. Several of Leaping Moon's friends moved to surround Jik. Jik reached into his pouch and spread open a cloak. He wrapped himself, the cloak expanding as he did it. By the time he was covered he wasn't there any longer. He had made himself invisible. Moving away from the camp, he had Caw watch the proceedings and report to him the outcome. He moved to a special hidden covacha cave only Dancing Fox knew about. Jik needed rest regardless of his powers, crawling into a bed of antelope skins he was soon sleeping without dreams. As twilight approached, Dancing Fox was able to slip away from the tribe and make her way to the secret cave. She brought jerked elk mixed with berries and herbs. Caw had alerted Jik before she arrived. He felt better, rested and alert. Leaping Moon tried to sneak up the mountainside barely avoiding a trap Jik had put out. It wouldn't have permanently injured anyone, but it would announce their presence. Caw flew from the cave, with a swarm of wasps to attack Leaping Moon. Dancing Fox watched in amazement as the warrior ran swatting and cursing. Her eyes gleamed with laughter as he disappeared. "The only way for Juan Two Raptors to prevail in council, is if I go away for a time," Jik told her. She knew this was right, but it didn't stop the tears from flowing down her cheeks. He captured a tear and held it to his lips. "I will return for you and your people when the time is right, I promise," he said. This didn't make it any easier for Dancing Fox. She stared into his eyes and touched his face as if to memorize everything about him. Jik walked Dancing Fox back to the village of the Apcuitl. He knew it might be the last time he stood amongst these good people. He also knew Leaping Moon waited in ambush for him. Taking his cloak from his pouch he disappeared, rather than hurt the young warrior. Three owls screeched and brushed their claws over Leaping Moon causing him to almost void his bladder in shame. Jik left his buckskin horse behind. He was still not sure of all of his powers, but his journey in search of his past, he sensed would not be easy. Climbing the steep cliffs behind the village in the dark cleared his head. Caw flew guard above watching for enemies. He climbed for hours before pulling brush over himself to block most of the wind, he fell asleep. The autumn days were warm as the yellow sun crept above the surrounding mountains, the smell of winter was in the air. The alkali desert lay east and south and he believed he must travel in those directions. Even though he knew Pig Tooth and his son, Shadow Tloz would try and kill and eat him. Then they would come after the Apcuitl. Shadow Tloz was perhaps more cunning than his father and Jik felt that he was better acquainted with the black arts. He reached into his pouch and drew forth a fist sized crystal. Looking deep into the glowing gemstone he saw the Navctl and the Athabascol tribes on the hunt. They were lifelong friends of the Apcuitl. He must tell them of the coming war and enlist their aid. Mule deer and antelope were being smoked and seasoned with chilies and salt and pinon nuts over a mesquite and spruce fire. A Brontosaurus was being roasted and the women were working on the skins. Jik could see this in his magic stone, as well as the enemy the Tlazolteot. Their hideous faces were painted and they were dancing around a captured warrior of the Navctl. Shadow Tloz was preparing to cut out his heart to share with his father and to add to his stature as the evil shaman of the Tlazolteot. There was no time for Jik to save the brave Navctl warrior; the distance was too great for him to attempt a rescue. He bowed his head in prayer and put away his seeing stone. He vowed that he would never let magic control his life, even though he was unaware of all his powers. Everything still remained a mystery and an experiment. He must know what he was capable of before challenging Pig Tooth and Shadow Tloz. Jik would never abandon his adopted people the Apcuitl. Dancing Fox was everything he wanted in a lady. At the moment he needed to know where he came from and why and how he came so close to death. Who had attacked him? Was there anyone waiting for him? He didn't fear death. Anyone could die, living was more difficult. Shadow Tloz plunged his blade into the throat of his captive; blood squirted high covering his face and upper torso. He howled and banshee screamed, his voice reverberating off the walls of stone near their encampment. The warriors were weaving and staggering from fermented xtabentin. Pig Tooth sat back watching his son whip the warriors, deviously into a maddening frenzy. Tomorrow with sore heads they would take the war to the Apcuitl. They would then discover the powers of the new sorcerer. The one that had the power to make sand swallow seventeen of his finest men. Pig Tooth hoped to squeeze the blood from his still beating heart, while looking him in the eyes. The Navctl was brave, but no man could endure the savagery of the Tlazolteot. Shadow Tloz stabbed and hacked the young captive. The heart and entrails were flung on a large crimson stained boulder encrusted with years of dried blood. The intestines and organs were cut into pieces and meted out to the dancing men. Penis and testicles were tossed to the women. They pretended to have sex with them, screaming in insane laughter. The head was kicked into the camp square where the now entirely naked tribe sucked out the eyeballs and brains, racing the swarms of flies before the squirming maggots took over. The sexual orgy was in wild abandonment, several of the men had sex with dogs and horses. Pig Tooth and Shadow Tloz retired to their shelter taking the cleanest women for their bidding. At daybreak the warpath awaited. Shadow Tloz vowed that when it was over and they had finally conquered the Apcuitl for all time, he would overthrow his father. Pig Tooth was getting fat and juicy. The night was a beautiful dream, the stars, pearl milky moon, wispy clouds, and fireflies swimming through oceans of darkness. The wind whispered and sang and snaked over the grasses into the valley below. Thunderbolts of annihilation shook Jik into the red fiendish grotesque maw of the lewd Tlazolteot. He felt himself being pulled into the gaping mouth of a hideous nightmare. It was a phantasmagoria of death everywhere. Only with extreme cunning would he be able to conquer the demon cannibals. In his mind's eye he could see the Tlazolteot using magic and shape shifting into gigantic black gray timber wolves tearing and rending enemies beyond decimation. They had suet where their heart should be located. Before the Tlazolteot could wait in ambush or take the attack to another tribe, Jik knew what he had to do. He sent Caw with many feathered friends aloft to scout for Pig Tooth and his men. Eagles and hawks soared high overhead riding the air, out of sight to the naked human eye. Jik pointed his metal rod at a big odd shaped stone. A mist of fog rolled around and a man appeared. He walked toward him smiling with open arms. Jik felt like he knew him, but he wasn't sure. "What a reception," scoffed the man. "I would expect something more cheerful from my own little brother." He pulled Jik into a hug. Jik was taken aback and not entirely trusting. Too much magic and things he didn't understand were happening to him at the moment. "You say you are my brother? What is your name and where did you come from? No one lives inside a stone." "My name is Ingeniso. I am not sure of the extent of your injuries or if your memory will ever come back entirely. The people that cared for you have done a superb job and we owe them great thanks. I am sorry that I was not able to contact you sooner, but other business detained me. I do not live in the stone, but I could think of worse places. When the time is right I will tell you where we come from and what our mission is." This was all said outright, but it still didn't detract from the mysterious message lying underneath. "I used the stone to travel, but that can be explained better with time. Now from what I can tell, you are about to become involved in a dangerous undertaking. I will not try to talk you out of it. You have always been rather headstrong." Ingeniso said with a smile. "But first a quick bite to eat, before we begin." He pulled out a handful of fire from the air and two pots. One contained, a liquid, that Jik was unfamiliar with, the other smelled like aquilops with sage. "How did you find me?" Jik asked his brother as they ate, the drink had a strengthening effect. "I've always known where you were. I have a seeing stone, like yours. I was on the other side of world and could not get to you until now. I knew you were in good hands and I could always protect you, even from afar. Our methods of travel can be quite fast. That's something else you will learn in time." "Do we have any other people nearby?" asked Jik. "Not at the moment," Ingeniso explained mysteriously. Jik didn't much care for all the secrecy from his supposed brother. He could not accept at face value this man even was his brother. There was just too much happening at the moment, to throw in another variable. Leaping Moon's followers met at the stream under the cover of darkness. They refused to wait for Black Knife and the elder's decision on seeking out the Tlazolteot. Since Jik had appeared, the tribe remained divided between peace and war. Even Juan Two Raptors, one of the fiercest fighters and warriors had voted for peace. Winter was also the enemy, driving them from the high country. Safety was to be had in the mountains. Their horses required grazing in the green valley's fed by melting snow. With Leaping Moon and almost half the warriors on the warpath, there would be fewer mouths to feed, but the hunters would have to make every shot count. Juan Two Raptors knew that Leaping Moon was making a huge mistake, dividing the fighting men of the tribe. There was always danger lurking and he'd never felt fear, but he felt responsible for the people he loved. Now was a time for peace. If war could be avoided, it should be at all costs. Deep in his heart he knew Jik would be watching over Leaping Moon and his men. Dancing Fox was smitten with this stranger and his uncle, Black Knife approved. Juan Two Raptors had never known him to have bad judgment, especially about his daughter. The Apcuitl left the mountains, joking and laughing on the trail. They felt like they were human turtles, their shells were their traveling homes. Dancing Fox kept a distant eye out for Jik. Her father watched her; an almost silent prayer escaped his whispering lips. Juan Two Raptors was everywhere at once, working like four men. The sooner they were settled into their camp, the faster the hunters could get food ready for winter. Ibex, theropods, archaepteryx, raptor, ducks, geese, aquilops, and smaller animals made up most of their diet. A few Stegosaurus were to be found on the plains and scouts and hunting parties were sent after them. Trout, catfish, gar, carp, and sturgeon were caught by a variety of methods. Small nets made with woven strips of willow, poles, spears, and the most fun way by hand. Flour was made with acorns, beaten cattail and yucca roots, mixed with rose hips and berries, this was made into bread and traveling food. Meat was hung from trees and smoked for days and salted and cured, when time allowed. Salt was traded for from tribes that lived near the land of the great salt water. Black Knife gave the order to make camp in a place just large enough for the people and animals. Everyone was exhausted from the trail. The evening stars soon greeted the smoke of their campfires. Suddenly scream after scream broke through the camp. The remaining warriors searched for attackers to no avail. Women and children were being strangled and decapitated by an invisible force. Death rode on a black whirlwind, sweeping up their heads and carrying them into the sky. Soon all the Apcuitl were silent. Hordes of rats and scavengers descended from the woods to feast on their blood and bones. Pig Tooth smiled at this evil revenge. Until their enemies were decimated they would never rest. The Tlazolteot had an ambush waiting for the remaining warriors. Leaping Moon never stood a chance against the powerful magic ambush set in place for him. Shadow Tloz had planned the extermination of all the Apcuitl. The first part of his plan had worked perfectly. Screaming bloody heads rained down on Leaping Moon and his warriors. The men recognized their wives' and children and they became transfixed. Gleams of a million lights sprang from the eyes of the decapitated heads, blinding the warriors. Supernatural monstrous Tyrannosaurus Rex roared and stripped the flesh from the confused men. They all died and were soon eaten, the lion's stomachs growing tight as drums. The head of Dancing Fox was deposited by a gust of wind at the feet of Jik. He knew he'd been distracted by the sorcerer, Shadow Tloz. The man wasn't his brother or friend. He had nothing left, but revenge, but he must recover first. Jik took his true love's head to give it a proper burial. Shadow Tloz had no need for the deception of Ingeniso's body, it melted and he stepped out of the smoldering pile of steaming smoking muck. Speaking in an evil sounding language of guttural glots, hicks, and humphs; known only by Pig Tooth and the devil minions they worshiped, he summoned the demon wrath. The stone he had deceivingly appeared from shot lightning bolts into Jik. The electricity seemed to feed and drain his energy. With his last remaining strength, Jik drew forth his magic rod; the earth vanished momentarily in a blinding explosion. He escaped with the remains of Dancing Fox. Waking up in strange surroundings with an echoing noise he had never heard before. Jik felt bizarre.

Romeo Van Gogh

It was too early for a beer, Romeo decided to study a few art history books about the female nudes, he loved to paint. The librarian looked exceptionally ravishing; she resembled Marilyn Monroe with the blue black hair of Cleopatra. She had book worm intelligence about her, what you might expect in a small village library. There was Mona Lisa laughter dancing behind her flirtatious radiant eyes. Her hair had a few strands of gray and her glasses gave her a studious appeal. Romeo's dark wavy hair, green blue intense penetrating eyes, sensuous smile, and slim muscular body usually had a positive effect on women. He asked her about books of beautiful naked women painted by Egon Schiele, Gustave Courbet, and Paul Gauguin. Romeo explained his desire to capture the face of a lady in the throes of an orgasm. He could tell this piqued her interest as she directed him to a small secluded area, where the books were located. It was unusually silent; he could hear a clock ticking on the wall. There was no one besides himself and the librarian in the building. The books he wanted were on the top shelves and out of reach. At the end of the aisle was a ladder with wheels connected to a rail, along the top and bottom of the bookcase. A sign on the wall read, For Librarian's Use Only. Romeo walked back to the desk to ask for assistance. The librarian was turned away from the counter, working bent over a stack of books. He checked out her figure. Her body was outstanding and extremely desirable. He could feel his member growing stiff as he cleared his throat to get her attention. 'Excuse me, Miss, I need you,' he said. She turned and raised an eyebrow in inquiry. 'There's a book I can't quite reach,' Romeo explained. She followed him without a word, back to the aisle in question. He pointed to the books he required. She slid the ladder down the rail and brushed against Romeo's huge growing erection, as she started up the ladder. She had long smooth legs, ending in black lacy panties. As she started back down, he ran one hand up the back of her thigh and with the other rubbed her wet pussy, massaging her clitoris and inserting a finger. She stopped above him on the last rung of the ladder and made a low purring cat like sound in the back of her throat. He rolled her panties down off one leg and she kicked them out of the way. Romeo lifted her skirt and cupped both cheeks of her ass, spreading her open. He put his tongue inside her vagina and teased and nibbled her clitoris, as she hunched him like there was no tomorrow. 'Not here, please, please, please, goddamn you,' she moaned. In the next breath she kept saying, 'Yes, yes, fuck yes,' over and over. She pulled Romeo's face into her drenched feverish pussy. Romeo dropped his pants and slowly lowered her down off the ladder on to his humongous throbbing penis. He impaled her and thrust for all he was worth, working in and out. Plunging left and right, deep and shallow, working like a maniac stallion jackhammer, he almost pulled all the way out, until she screamed for more. He removed her shirt and bra, Romeo's tongue and mouth tantalized her perfect breasts and beautiful nipples. She became almost uncontrollable; her hair came undone and grew wilder by the second. Books and shelves rattled with a frenzied earthquake rhythm. So far, they hadn't been discovered. The librarian's eyes glazed over in pleasure and passion, but there was also a hint of terror. Romeo locked this face in his memory for a painting later as they finished, in a nearly collapsing mutual orgasm. Feeling a bit worn out, but far from entirely satiated, they fixed their clothes and he left to get his oil paints and canvas. The librarian decided to close the library early for her appointment to pose for Romeo. Unbridled lust engulfed her mind, body, and soul like a mountain torrential rain storm sending walls of water down the dry arroyos of the desert. Her thighs and nipples trembled and throbbed as she thought of Romeo.

Frida Kahlo

First time I met my great Uncle Woodrow Wilson Vann he was in the hospital getting his left foot amputated at the ankle because of a diabetes infection. My grandmother, his youngest sister and I traveled to the panhandle of Oklahoma from New Mexico to say goodbye. I was ten years old. I'd heard a lot about Uncle Woodrow, he was a scallywag. He was a self-taught musical genius, playing guitar, violin, mandolin, banjo, accordion, and piano. Woodrow put food on the table playing at dances, fairs, and in churches. The Vann family was mostly Cherokee and Choctaw. They moved from Tennessee to Oklahoma in a covered wagon. Later they moved south down on the Rio Grande River to Presidio, Texas during Prohibition. Woodrow learned Spanish and would swim across the river and play mariachi and norteno music, and then bring back tequila and mescal. He would tie the liquor bottles up in a sack and put the rope around his neck and swim back north. Uncle Woodrow was on his death bed when we arrived, but was hanging on to life by his fingernails. He wadded and twisted up his sheets into a knot and tried to stuff them into his mouth like chewing tobacco. Woodrow yelled and thrashed about like a captured alligator, scaring me and lots of folks.

My grandmother and I went to Turkey Creek to stay with her oldest sister, Aunt Bertie. Her hillbilly grandsons taught me about using the outhouse and looking out for spiders and snakes, since they had no running water. They took me fishing, taught me how to call a turkey, and how to bark squirrels; shooting a single shot 22 into the tree bark near the squirrel to knock it cold, without damaging the meat for the frying pan. The boys thought I was a real city slicker and took me to the barbershop to get a haircut from a blind barber. I looked like I was ready to enlist in the army; they thought that was real funny.
A few days later we went back to visit Uncle Woodrow and they

had amputated his right leg at the hip. He died soon after that and we stayed for the funeral. When the funeral home went to collect Woodrow's body, it had disappeared. No one had an explanation. It's been fifty years since I've thought about this because I came across some old black and white photos of him wearing his sombrero and the post cabin the Vann's had built down in Texas. The cedar posts were driven deep vertical rather than horizontal with viga posts laid atop for the roof beams. I plan on scanning and including photos of this true story.

Sometimes I think the ghost of Uncle Woodrow sort of took up residence in my soul. I've always loved everything Mexican, I learned Spanish, went to Mexico every chance I got, and have been married to a Mexican beauty for thirty years. My lady and I travel often to Guadalajara, the second biggest city in Mexico. Her family moved there from Mexico City when she was thirteen, she was the youngest of eight children. Her father was an accountant, a land owner, and a liquor store inspector in Mexico City. After they moved her mother started a restaurant called The Bonanza, in Guadalajara, it was frequented by firemen and policemen.

We went to Mexico City often to visit her many relatives that lived there. Her Tio Francisco was a captain in the Mexican police force and ended up in the Mexican equivalent to the F.B.I. He studied under J. Edgar Hoover and once caught a famous French jewel thief. Due to his high government position we were able to visit Los Pinos (The Pines) which is Mexico's White House and see many government buildings that are off limits to the public. We saw huge murals done by Diego Rivera, where he met Frida Kahlo. He supposedly was high upon some scaffolding, painting and he told some girls to go get him cerveza and tequila and they refused. Frida was among them; Diego took out his pistol and fired at them like they were cucarachas.

Magdalena Carmen Frieda Kahlo y Calderon born: July 6th, 1907 died July 13th, 1954. She had polio at age 6, making one leg thinner than the other. On Sept 17th, 1925 she was on a bus that hit a trolley car, an iron handrail pierced her abdomen and uterus. She received a broken spinal column, collar bone, ribs, and pelvis. She became pregnant three times, but was never able to have children. Frida met Diego in 1927 and they married in 1929.

I became enraptured by Frida Kahlo, her sad interesting life and her beautiful curious paintings. One of the things that magnetically and magically drew me to her was her having her leg amputated due to gangrene not long before she died. I always thought about her and Uncle Woodrow having the same infirmity. We would visit La Casa Azul, the Blue House that she shared with Diego, Her father built the house. Leon Trotsky and his wife lived there for a while to escape, Joseph Stalin. Frida had an affair with Trotsky and he moved nearby to a fortress like house and was assassinated three years later in 1940. Both of their houses were turned into museums. Diego died three years after Frida and left their house to the government.

In 1938, Andre Breton called Frida, "a ribbon around a bomb." Frida and Diego got divorced in 1939, after she discovered Diego was having an affair with her younger sister, Christina. They remarried in 1940. Frida was a bisexual; she had affairs with Josephine Baker and Isamu Noguchi. Her painting, The Suicide of Dorothy Hale from 1939, always affected me, I'd seen a lady fall from a tall building and splatter on a sidewalk, and it was almost identical to what she captured on her canvas and bloody frame.

After several visits to The Frida Museum we got to know the Coyoacan neighborhood of Mexico City. There were many ceramic tile and pottery shops filled with ornate tile and pottery of all kinds. The Tolstoy Museum was within walking distance of

La Casa Azul. It was a surreal wonderful adventure to explore the entire area.

My lady's other Uncle was a foreman in a bullet factory and lived next to a huge bullfighting arena. Tio Luis had a daughter named Juanita. She was a soap opera star and drop dead gorgeous. Her breathtaking beauty stopped traffic, men and women's heads swiveled. She looked like a cross between Liz Taylor and Sophia Loren. Juanita invited us to the nearby volcano mountains, Iztaccihuatl, Mujer Dormida or the sleeping woman and to Popocatepetl, the brave warrior. The mountains resembled what the Nahuatl people had named them for. After the panoramic views and hairpin turn roads in the mountains, Juanita suggested we have dinner at Xochimilco, the Venice of Mexico City complete with gondolas covered in flowers.

Between the canals were many islands with adobe and thatch houses. Joyful people, with chickens, pigs, dogs, cats, turkeys, even horses, and cows lived there. I saw hammocks strung between trees and heard music and singing. It was a happy place, a place of love. My lady and her cousin were in one end of the gondola and I was in the other end with the boatman. Some turkeys were at the edge of water drinking. I let loose with a turkey call I'd learned long ago. The turkeys answered excitedly, lots of them started gobbling. People from the island and boats wanted to see what all the commotion was about. I almost had a turkey riot on my hands, the boatman was laughing so hard he almost fell in the water.

A tall man came out of the shadows and said, "I think you learned that call in Turkey Creek." He winked at me and hugged his woman close. I looked and it was my Uncle Woodrow Wilson with Frida Kahlo, they were alive, smiling, and had two good legs.

The Same Rifle That Killed JFK

Jarhead and I hunted America and Mexico for forty years. It was delicious like opening a frosty can of Coors, but it got too easy. Gunpowder took away the sport. We tried blowguns, spears, throwing sticks, and settled on slingshots. It took five years before we killed a deer with a rock. My lady, Juanita wanted to experience the hunt. She carried an old Italian Carcano army rifle I'd bought in an Army Surplus store on the cheap. We helped her find a good spot at the top of a hill and spread out. A herd of deer appeared like silent magic, a twelve point buck leading. We had our rocks ready to fly, but we held fire letting Juanita take her first shot at a living creature. Just as the deer were disappearing, BOOM. The antlers of the buck caved towards each other like felled Sequoias. One shot in a million.

Hippopotamus Summer

She'd lived four summers and loved Snake Alley Noodles, Delaware Punch, strawberry ice cream, and the wildflowers that grew along the railroad tracks, which divided the old celery fields of West Milwaukee. Different kinds of flowers grew each summer, purple coneflowers, ox-eye sunflowers, blue lobelia, Jacob's ladder, and black-eyed Susan, their seeds mostly planted by birds and animals. The last two summers, wild crazy red, yellow, and orange sunflowers conquered the hippopotamus colored steel tracks. Their green stalks and roots war snaked down through the black goo creosote coated railroad ties. The tracks took me back forty years to an all- night walk across the vast Ft. Worth, Texas to catch a west bound freight for home in New Mexico. Stumbling over ankle spraining rocks and gravel and jumping into the prickly pear and yucca to avoid getting creamed by an Atchison, Topeka, and Santa Fe express. My young daughter wanted to get a few flowers for her mom. We stopped at the store for a few items and I pulled around back to the loading dock area, where there was a jungle of flowers. I thought this is a thirty second job and opened my pocket knife and asked her to remain in the cool car. I got out and was almost done when I felt the tug of a small hand on my shirt. There was my daughter with a big smile that pulled and stretched my heart half way to Tucumcari. The car was running with the keys locked inside. I noticed a semi-truck with another behind it waiting to use the dock. I grabbed my daughter's little hand and told the truck drivers I'd need to call my lady for an extra set of keys, they were not happy. Fifteen minutes later, mom came to the rescue and we got out of our predicament. That was twenty years ago, I've seen Van Gogh's sunflowers in Arles since, but none compare to the beautiful memories of my ladies and the hippopotamus summer.

Pluck

After making friends with Maya on face book I figured she wouldn't mind a visit. I found out where she lived and jumped on a southbound Greyhound. The worst part was avoiding peeing on myself in the skinny bathroom while hitting potholes. When the dog arrived, I stopped at Popeye's and got us a bucket of crispy chicken and the fixings. I rang her doorbell and a man that resembled a black Adolf Hitler answered, he wouldn't let me enter until I gave him a thigh and neck bone from the fowl. When I saw the queen of poetry I smiled and gave her some fried okra with a packet of hot sauce. She looked me over from head to toe, her eyes seemed magnetic. Finally she spoke. "I'll bet you're pure hell on the ladies." I said, "I do alright." She removed her drawers and said, "Let's see what you can do you silver-tongued devil." I plunged in all the way to my ears, she started moaning and groaning and carrying on. I got a bit frightened, I thought I was going to fucking kill her. She started whistling and pulling my hair out by the roots. I figured she had enough. "Goddamn. You sure got a lot of pluck for a naked neck rooster scalawag." I put my crotch in her face and asked, "Do you fetch bone?" "I'm too old to be your bitch, now give me the rest of that chicken and get the hell out of here." I hit the bricks back to the bus station.

The Ants

I was watering the apple tree and these ants parachuted onto my arm and started biting the shit out of me. I slapped them, but for every one I crushed, two more ants replaced them. My arm started swelling up like a fire hydrant. They spoke to each other in ant language and said, "This is the motherfucker that burned us with a magnifying glass when he was a kid, quite the serial killer. Let's bite his goddamn arm off." Those were some mean ass ants with long memories. Now I'm known as Lefty.

Defacing the Mail

The post office let all the clerks be mail carriers for one day. My assignment was to drive around and empty all the deposit boxes in a certain section of the city. So I followed my map and went from box to box and emptied all the letters and small packages into the back of the blue jeep. It was mundane, but it got me out of the building for a change.

I'm driving along and I see a shapely brunette walking a small dog. She waves me down and asks for a ride. I know this is against regulations, but I like her pink toenails. "Hop in babe," I tell her. She has her dog on her lap, her blue dress starts scooting up her long legs. I soon figure out she has no panties on. I grab the dog and toss it in back, so I can get a better view. Looking in back the dog is pissing all over the mail.

"Do you want to bury your bone?" she asks, as she plays with herself. I pull over on a shady stretch of pavement. She's got her tits out and dress up and yanks my pants around my ankles. The dog takes a shit on somebody's birthday card. I get it in and start really working and this giant rat jumps out of nowhere and grabs the dog by the throat. The dog is getting murdered and the woman is screaming and this just turns me on more. I'm trying to bust both nuts into heaven. The woman and what's left of the dog jump out of the jeep, half naked and attempts to beat on the rat. The rat jumps back in the jeep, landing on my dick, clawing and chewing and I erupt all over everything.

The woman starts running down the street, but drops the dog. I try to chase her down, but end up running over the dog, killing it. I gather up the dog waffle and later throw it in a mailbox I had emptied before. The woman is a ghost.

I figure, I've fucked a beauty, got blown by a rat, made breakfast out of a dog and mailed it. In the process I committed, the number one postal sin, defacing the mail. I drove back to the post office.

The dock boss asked me how was my day.

"It was kind of boring, but not too bad."

Hot Pussy

My lady's female friends always came over for gab fests and ate all our food and drank most of our beverages, which irritated me. The worst thing was they stayed until late into the night and took forever to say goodbye. They were always going to the bathroom to powder their noses, so to speak.

This gave me a brilliant devious idea on how to cut their visits short. I went on line to the Lava Co. and ordered Thai Dragon Powder and Bhut Jolokia Red Powder, two of the hottest peppers there are. I diluted the powders with flour and rubbed them in a roll of toilet paper before my lady's next party. I hung my trap and waited for the results. It wasn't long before most of the women were squirming and corkscrewing, trying to dry rub their burning crotches on the couch. They were soon grabbing their purses and heading for the door. I was trying to hide my ear to ear grin from my quizzical lady. She knew something was up, but couldn't quite figure it out. When she went upstairs for her shower, I switched the paper and got rid of the burning evidence and scrubbed the toilet seat.

I sat down and laughed like hell and read my book by Pearl Sydenstricker Buck, The Good Earth. I couldn't help pondering why John and Martha Truman named their son, Harry S. and the S. stood for absolutely nothing.

Under the Atlantic

A British man with a name I'd never heard sent poems to a blog site I jointly run. He said he was in Spain caring for a sick dog, I had an eerie feeling something supernatural was happening. His girlfriend was trying to help him to return to England. He figured he'd crash with his parents and work as a gardener and write. I called him and said I was on my way to Paris for a reading and to meet a French publisher that accepted my sex novella. The Frenchman said he tried reading it on the bus, but he kept getting a hard on. My pal said in England they call it an erection on, also the American's use of the word cunt was frowned upon. I finished the marijuana joint I was smoking and wrote him and said, "Cunt and hard on is bad?" He just laughed as I hung up.

After taking several Xanax and slurping martinis I killed my panic about flying. I saw the Eiffel Tower from a taxi, but I was still very fucked up on the way to my hotel. I did my reading at The Shakespeare & Co. Bookstore, I sold a few chapbooks and talked a bit of smack. My pal was sitting there grinning. I didn't know it was him until he introduced himself. He told me the dog died and he had buried it in his friend's backyard, but something had dug it up in the night. He suggested taking the Chunnel train to London before I was to head back to America, I agreed.

We had a few beers and smoked a blunt of hash mixed with tobacco before boarding the train. It was a two hour trip by high speed rail. We were an hour under the water when the train stopped and all the lights went out. I felt anxiety crawling up the back of my throat like a caterpillar with gonorrhea, especially when I saw my British pal being attacked by a red eyed demon zombie dog from Spain. I took off my shoe started beating on the canine and screamed a Mexican Indian cure chant. It must have had some effect, the lights flickered and the dog vanished.

I ordered a bottle of gin and poured my pal a few stiff drinks. We were both tanked by the time we hit Great Britain, but at least we were still breathing. Spanish dog zombies are sure as fuck not man's best friend.

Juarez, Mexico

Growing up four hours north of the Mexican border had its advantages, besides taking mandatory Spanish from the first grade on. There was legal drinking, semi-legal weed, and inexpensive prostitutes, if you could hang onto your wallet and stay alive, just to the south. When I was fifteen, my older brother invited my amigo and I to tag along to Juarez to party and get our cherries popped. After four hours of Grand Funk, the Doors, and Steppenwolf in the back of his 58 Chevy we were ready to stretch our legs, all three of them.

We entered a cantina that looked like Emiliano Zapata and Pancho Villa armed to the teeth complete with cartridge belts across their chests had just vacated. The senoritas migrated toward our table, they were all ages and sizes. We ordered several bottles of mezcal with the worm inside attempting to swim the Rio Grande. A girl not much older than me sat on my lap and had soon coaxed a stiff reception out of totem pole. My friend and I were led into a backroom behind a multicolored blanket. An old lady wanted to do a pecker check for disease, she'd been patting out corn tortillas over a charcoal fire. She had us drop our laundry and proceeded to milk our dicks to see if any yellow discharge was dripping or any crabs were doing the mambo. Her hands felt good and warm, I saw my pal shoot his wad right in her face. He had to pay the mamasita more than me for his liquid donation. Our chosen ladies soon came back and led us into a room with two twin beds, they made us remove our clothes. The lights went out and we were in total darkness. I felt sticky sprayed hair brushing my chest and something wet and cool enveloping my penis. It had an up and down gyrating motion, but didn't feel like a vagina to me. It seemed more like a plastic bag full of tortilla lard. This did nothing for me and I soon pushed the lady away. My buddy did the same, we paid the whores and agreed to lie to my brother and his pals about how wonderful it had been.

A month later, my girlfriend and I got in the backseat of my 55 Chevy Bel Air. Under a violet blue deep roasted sky dripping milky stars, I looked into her butterscotch eyes and we had our way with each other. I heard recently she has a pizza joint in Denver, which should be a great business now that marijuana is cool there.

From our trip to Mexico, my brother caught the seven year itch. He almost went crazy, until we went to Roswell, New Mexico to rebuild a bowling alley that got destroyed by a tornado. An old doctor examined him and looked at his hands under a microscope and said he had scabies. The medicine he got made him scream and dance, my dad and I got a few good laughs about that.

Hazel Blue Rat Malaria

Driving a truck at the university wasn't bad. Starting off every morning with a fat joint, then cruising and checking out the young flesh was great. Freshly scrubbed, bouncing boobies, strutting their stuff with those firm long legs. The money wasn't colossal, but the panoramas and fringe benefits were outstanding.

First job of the day was; go to the lab dock of the science building and pick up all the monkey, rabbit, mouse, frog, and rat manure. Take it to the compacting dumpster, throw in the double bags, and push the button for the ram to cram it into the huge metal container.

That particular morning my mind was in my pants, thinking about a lovely lady. I pushed the button and this gigantic hairy gray rat with red beady eyes jumped out of the dumpster and hit me right in the face and chest. The filthy rodent must have been the size of a small dog. I stumbled backwards almost tripping, my heart felt like a jackhammer trying to escape my body.
Still shaking I drove to a bar and drank four double vodkas with beer chasers, before I felt my nerves get back under control. Walking unsteadily to the men's room, I saw a trickle of blood where the rat nicked me in the throat with a claw. Scrubbing the wound with soap, I went back and soaked my neck with vodka, inside and out.

The next morning after my doober and nookie lookee, I picked up a load of dung. The sky was hazel blue and tulips of saffron and crimson swayed in the spring breeze. Bumble bees buzzed and bumbled. Life was honey. The last few nights I'd balled this nympho law student from Amarillo. She was blonde and built well and very vocal about her orgasms. She liked to wear sweaters and nothing else. I reiterate, honey.

Figuring the rats had acquired a liking for their relative's poop, I decided to use a different dumpster. I lowered the tailgate on my truck and hopped up to the bed to begin unloading. I threw in the first bag.

"Hey, wait a minute damn it," croaked a wino scrambling out of the dumpster hitching his pants up. When he got clear I threw in another bag. "Wait mister," he held up his hand. A bag woman climbed out and grinned wickedly at me.

"We were just having a little fun. I'll polish your knob for three dollars. How about it?" she said.

"Maybe another time."

"Okay sugar," she winked and waggled her ass at me.

I looked up at a cloud passing in front of the sun and felt feverish. "Hey wait a minute," I heard myself yell.

Eating Raw Jackrabbit and Snorting Black Cocaine

"You want a blow job or a piece of ass?" It sounded like Julio was reading from a sex menu. I could see his crooked demented grin.

"Here you go vato. Take your pick." He threw two burlap sacks at me. In one was the head of his bitchy girlfriend. In the other was her ass, with the pussy still attached by meat and tendons. I went to puke my guts out in his bathtub. He laughed like a fucking insane hyena, picking up bloody remains and tossing them in his piranha tank. I finished projectile vomiting in the fish bowl almost getting my face ripped off, by those snapping jumping motherfuckers.

I'd had the worst dream of my life the night before, after drinking El Cheapo tequila. This big hairy tarantula was sliding up and down my erect dick, singing Christmas songs and it felt so damn good, I decided to quit the human race. Then I passed some wicked gas and killed the spider, my one true love.

My Uncle Benny drove up in his shit can Ford and wanted to go hunting out of season. "We can always go bump off some bunny rabbits and make a pot of stew. Don't waste your lead on jackrabbits, them motherfuckers are tougher than a buffalo dick. Stick to cottontails, they're nice and juicy." I was glad to get away from Julio; he was seriously fucked in the brain from the war.

We drove into the country for about a half hour near little stream. I rolled us a couple of pinner doobies. I took a toke and a jackalope sized rabbit jumped up, I blew off its ears and scalped its brain. My Uncle just shook his head, he knew it was a great shot, but I hadn't listened to his advice. He took my shit because I was the only one in our family of the third generation to get

an Honorable Discharge from the army. No other game even
showed up that day. We took the rabbit home, but by this time
I had the marijuana munchies. I sliced, diced, and slapped that
jackrabbit on a flour tortilla with several sloshes of hot sauce and
garlic salt and ate that bad boy like a filet mignon. I had a couple
of grams of black rock coca from Lima, Peru a pal had gotten
from the Shining Path guerrillas. I cut a few lines, by this time
Uncle Benny was a willing participant. We got seriously wasted
and scored some cowgirls down at the cantina, after beating their
ass playing pool. We danced and romanced them back to my crib.

That morning looking out my window under an indigo bluebird
sky, I saw this huge fat familiar female ass jammed and stuck in
a window frame, where glass once existed. There was a dribble
of blood where the glass had cut bitten that butt. When the fire
truck and paramedics arrived it looked like an R-rated Three
Stooges show. A crowd was gathering by eleven, somebody
pulled out a couple of forties of malt liquor, another had a pint of
rotgut whiskey. Laughter filled the air, as they pried that big ass
out of the window.

"That motherfucker tried to kill me. You ask if I want press
charges, look at that smug son of a bitch, over there sucking
down hooch. He can't keep a job or a hard on, what good is he? I
might be fat, but I'm good and tight. Just ask that asshole staring out the window?" She pointed directly at me. I sort of did the
turtle move pulling back from the curtains. Uncle Benny laughed
and his cowgirl farted like a bullfrog and then mine joined in like
a serenade from the bayou. I turned the television on to a show
about Paul Gauguin and Pablo Picasso.

Last Comanchero of Dildo Island

Juanito was listening to The Rolling Stones song Star Fucker, it sounded like Johnny B. Goode with some curse words thrown in. He had John Fucking Wayne on the boob tube killing Indians and Mexicans from a flaming wagon traveling hell bent for leather across Monument Valley. I thought oh shit, here it comes, Juanito got out his Chicago typewriter case, unpacked his Thompson submachine gun and laid four hand grenades on the coffee table. Every time The Duke killed a Comanchero, he played like he was obliterating his cowboy ass, complete with mouth made burp gun sound effects and grenades with the pin left in, rolled under the television. "Did I ever tell you that I'm a direct descendant of Quanah Parker, the last wild half Comanche?"

"Only more times than I count," I replied.

"Well fuck you then, I won't waste my breath on a common asshole New Mexican." He fired up a joint and it started popping and fire was falling all over his shirt.

"Did you forget to take out the seeds and stems?"

"That's boogers and cunt hairs from a nun, I threw in for flavor," he explained. "Did you go out with that Canadian lady again? The one that says 'Give me a dozen beers' instead of a twelve pack. Her eyes are deeper than a blue jay fart. I wish she had a twin sister," Juanito said.

"Claudia is a combination of an angel, a Tasmanian she devil in the sack, and a glamorous old time Hollywood movie star. Do you feel me?"

"Yea, it's all good, you lucky motherfucker. You can step in a pile of dog shit up to your ankle and still come out smelling like a petunia."

I took several tokes and held them in. "You want to hear my latest poem?" Juanito nodded in assent.

Your Bootie's Now A Coochie

Oh funky freaky Frankenstino
another writer wannabeno
a stinky nobody nigarette
sucking dick on a cigarette

Time exposes fakes and frauds
go back down on your greasy broad
spewing vain and volatile words
jealousy and breathing slimy turds

Just another snake in the grass
Big Willy is gonna fuck yo ass
being his jail bitch was unacceptable
he passed you around for a sperm receptacle.

"Is this about the fucker that pissed you off, writing about your wife and kid on the web and he'd never really written jackshit of his own?"

I nodded. "It got personal, when he brought family into the equation. He reminds me of a fiddle player I used to know, named Ollie. I started out liking him, but he thought he was hot shit and kept running off at the mouth. One night I told Ollie to shut his pie hole. He had this long goatee and I grabbed it and hit him in the schnozzola. He fell straight back and farted, once like a foghorn and again like a dying bullfrog. I looked in my fist and I was holding what seemed like a handful of cunt hair ripped off a bushy snatch. I wasn't sure what to do with it, so I stuffed it in his mouth and went back in the bar to shoot some nine ball. His band was looking for him to play another set of music. Ollie finally staggered back inside, looking a little ragged."

"You're a crazy son of a bitch, but you know that already. I bet they don't realize that factoid."

"I just hope I never run into either punkass or I may just be forced to do something they won't appreciate. Are we going to score that fucking knock your dick in the dirt weed or whistle Dixie?"

"Vamanos, cabron."

We got in his lime green Ford F-100 pickup with the souped up engine, in case of trouble and went to our rendezvous. The dealer had two body guards, but we were loaded for bear and very cautious. He said it was Acapulco Gold, but that was salesman bullshit most of the time used to boost the price. I held a zip lock plastic sandwich bag of herb up to the light. It appeared to be mostly tops without much leafy shake. The tops were much more potent, but a lot of stems were left after stripping them down. I opened the bag and plunged my nose and mouth in, it smelled like a freshly cleaned horse barn with a pungent sweet twist of tree sap. I passed the baggie to Juanito, the aromatic odor was a delight to both our highly trained nostrils. He picked out one of the tightly golden compacted buds, it was woven through with light green leaves traced with reddish fiber veins. The bud was gummy to the touch, Juanito smiled and handed it to me, my fingers detected the sticky sensation. I squeezed the bud and a golden fully mature seed rolled out, none of those little green-white birdseeds. I flipped out some Zig-Zags and twisted up a pinner doobie. It wouldn't do to let the dealer know our enthusiasm over this ganja. Juan fired a wooden kitchen match and let the sulpher burn off, before adding flame to the smoke. The pot was pure fucking dynamite. Kilos were $80, the dude from Mexico gave us a deal because we bought ten, $750.

I knew for a fact the potent marijuana was coming in by box car from El Paso, Texas, smuggled by wetbacks. It was grown in the Sierra Madre Mountains in Sinaloa, Mexico on what farmers called their tomato plantations. It was a sweet deal and I had plenty of friends for breaking down and distributing my large purchases into a big money making operation. Juanito wasn't happy with his share of the profits, even though we were fifty/fifty partners, he was always a greedy motherfucker. He started cutting his weed with catnip, the elusive elixir for felines. We didn't get any complaints at first, but it just didn't feel right to me. Slowly I started ending our business venture together. His customers just weren't getting as good a buzz as mine.

Finally I had enough. "I'm going to Isla Mujeres off the Mexican Yucatan Peninsula and let things cool down."

"I'm headed north to Dildo Island, Newfoundland. I'm going to get me an Eskimo woman and live in an igloo," Juanito said.

I thought yea right, he's full of shit. He went north before I went south and he called me. "I've got me a nice lady, her name is Lucille, just like B.B. King's guitar. Here talk to her." He put her on the line, but neither of us had much to say.

The day before I was to split, Lucille called and told me Juanito had been eaten by a Polar bear.

Little Vietnam, Tigerland Fort Polk, Louisiana

"See that boot?" the drill sergeant bellowed.

"Yes, sir."

"I'm not a fucking officer, never call me sir."

"Give me twenty push-ups and kiss the tip of my boot twenty times."

"Yes, drill sergeant."

I could see my sweating reflection in his spit shined boots. Many alternatives briefly crossed my mind. Then I dropped and followed orders.

The drill sergeant wore a Smokey the Bear hat and was puffing on a stinky-assed stogie. He was a muscled throw back to the caveman days. I thought about shoving a grenade up his ass.

"Wipe the black off your lips. You look like you've been sucking on something rotten. Then report to the gas chamber." A nasty grin split his coal black face, his teeth were rat shit yellow.

The gas chamber was an old barracks with two horse troughs in front. You wore a full field pack, carried your weapon, and wore your steel helmet and gas mask. Two drill instructors made you run around the room until you were breathing hard, then they opened four canisters of mace and pepper gas. The room turned foggy and ate at any exposed skin like acid. They ordered us to halt, remove our helmets and hold them between our knees, remove our gas masks and replace our helmets on our heads.

The gas chewed at our eyes, nose, and mouth like a horde of stinging wasps on fire. The masked instructors smiled and slowly asked our name, rank, and where we were from. By this time most of us were foaming in froth like rabid dogs. We crawled outside to wash in the horse troughs, they were filled with piss and vomit.

One soldier dropped his helmet, he was ordered to return to the gas chamber the next day. That night he hung himself in the latrine.

Tigerland at Fort Polk, Louisiana was the closest thing to hell and Vietnam there was in America.

In July 1971, I celebrated my eighteenth birthday there, by digging a hole with my entrenching tool, my hands bled through blisters. Mosquitoes, chiggers, ticks, and deer flies swarmed and swam in your sweat and tried to burrow into your eyes and every orifice.

"I killed three men, with that little shovel, caved their skulls into hamburger," the drill sergeant bragged. We'd just eaten greasy canned meat, chunks of squash, and lumpy potatoes for lunch.

"What's wrong, boy? You usually got something stupid to say."

"It's my birthday and I was wondering how it feels to die," I replied.

"I'll tell you when it's your birthday, you are my child now. I am your mama, papa, and God. And if you want to know how it feels to die, I have three more weeks to teach you. Now, dig me a hole, you piece of shit."

"Yes, drill sergeant."

The concrete floors in the barracks were dyed red, so every item of white clothing soon ended up pink. Every pore of my body seemed to ooze Louisiana pink.
We went to the hand grenade pits the next day. We received a two hour lecture and demonstration on how to pull the pin and throw it. It's destructive force and five seconds before it would explode and blow the hell out of anything around. We had a three foot high cement wall to hide behind after throwing the grenade. There were three pits, divided by walls. Each had a hole in the corner in case someone just dropped it. A drill instructor was supposed to kick the live grenade down the hole, in case of accident. This duty was for instructors that had pissed someone higher up off.

Two southern boys were chosen to throw grenades at the same time as me. The first grenade toss went okay, but gravel pelted us from the sky. The drill instructor grinned. The second toss, the guy next to me couldn't get the pin out. The instructor went to help. They got the pin out, but juggled the grenade, just as the instructor kicked it toward the hole, it went off. His foot was gone, it looked like night crawlers spurting blood from his ankle. The southern boy was holding his ears, blood was pumping from his mouth and nose. His screams turned into red bubble gurgles.

Learning to kill was a bitch.

On completion of our seventh week of training, with one week to go, we were given three day passes. A Texan, an Arizonian, and a New Mexican (me) headed for New Orleans; head shaved G.I. Joe specials. We hit Bourbon Street and whored and drank and smoked weed. Fuck the army! We "borrowed" a car and cruised with some young nightingales and wound up in jail. The army came and got us, we were their property. We watched from a latrine window, which we were cleaning with toothbrushes, as all the other soldiers marched in the graduation parade. They were all decked out in dress green uniform and shiny.

We were recycled, eight weeks all over again, same old shit different day. All the Basic Training (boot camp) graduates got orders for specialized Army Individual Training and then were shipped onto Vietnam. We peeled potatoes, dug holes, got gassed, tossed grenades, and got inspected like cattle daily. By the time we graduated, Nixon had decided to send no more fresh American meat to Nam. They say every cloud has a silver lining, well sometimes even fucking up does too.

Lipstick on a Pig

I felt like Samson getting shorn by Delilah when I finally agreed to a six month boot camp rehab for my alcohol and drug problems. I was long over do, since I was losing my job and pension, all my friends in the world and small press, books, money and clothes, none of it mattered except my wife and daughter. I needed my ladies like oxygen, they were and are my reason to continue. I'd failed civilian rehabilitation many times and AA. Serving three long years in the army helped me get a house and job, now I needed to get clean. Turning to the Veteran's Administration Hospital for damaged soldiers, I learned the hard way what the Stockholm syndrome meant. There is no cure for alcoholism, my drug of choice, along with plenty of other seriously bad habits, but with training and perseverance, you can relearn how to be human a day at a time.

My first night I had nicotine withdrawals, there was no smoking until you earned that privilege. I could've used a few cowboy cigarettes rolled from butts or a bowl of smoke or snort to take the edge off. Nightmares of cartoons made me sweat, mainly Captain Kangaroo spanking a bare assed Mr. Green Jeans bent over his lap, while Bunny Rabbit's skinned and eviscerated body turned into shish kabob with raining carrots rotated over a glowing fire, it was crazy and invaded my sleep. I'd lost everything I owned, what I did have fit in a brown paper bag. I woke up and couldn't find my only pair of underwear, I'd washed in the sink and draped over the radiator to dry. I was sharing a room with three other guys. I saw this fat fucker in the next bed wearing my thirty six inch waist boxers around his forty four inch tub of lard. The elastic was a goner and his nuts were all squished. Deciding to donate my drawers to him, I figured going commando was better than getting cooties off his nasty ass. He rolled over and

I grabbed the back of my ex-Fruit of the Looms and gave him an atomic wedgie that looked like a man g-string. He was not a happy camper, but neither was I.

Having a few more hours to sleep, I dreamed of Libby Casper. She was red haired with creamy skin and a great body and she loved to tease the boys. Libby must've watched a movie with Gypsy Rose Lee, because she knew how to bump and grind to the music. Her parents had this monstrous aquarium full of goldfish. After a hot make out session, Libby told me she'd do a striptease and remove an item of clothing every time I swallowed a goldfish. There was a tiny net and I tried to capture the little fish, they weren't bad to swallow being all slick they went right down. A couple of them started squirming in my mouth and I spit them out and this got Libby even more excited. Her pancake sized boobs were topped with nice strawberry nipples. When she got down to her panties, I thought our game was over, but she said if I ate a big goldfish and chewed it up, she'd go all the way. I started coming out of my dream, feeling something wet on my face, it smelled like gas and I thought Libby's dad had punched me and was soaking me down to torch me. It was the fat dickhead wringing out my old underwear. I hit him hard in his two inch penis and tiny balls; they disappeared crawling right inside his body like magic. He screamed like Little Richard and went down like twenty pounds of shit in a ten pound sack.

We started our classes run by ex-drill instructors. One hundred eighty alcohol, narcotic, and cocaine anonymous meetings in ninety days and some were pure hell. We had physical education, art and crafts, lectures about parenting, about being a good civilian; we learned bridge, and played pool, dominoes, and chess. There were meetings with medical doctors, lawyers, musicians, nurses, and therapists. The program was five to six months and every aspect of the veteran's life was under the microscope. You were treated with dignity and could smoke tobacco and leave the grounds after the first two weeks. You were subject to random urine tests for any and all substance abuse, one failure and you were out of the program.

Most of the guys were black and they'd been sent north from Hines V. A. in Chicago, many were graduates from the Cook County Jail. They were real hard ass dudes that had lived under bridges and knew lots of hustles to stay alive. There were plenty of fights, but nobody wanted to go back to the streets, so they were over quickly. The job training programs were great. My job was waiting, if I could graduate and get clean and stay that way. I scored a temporary volunteer job in the old library built during the Civil War by Abe Lincoln. I taught men to get on the computers and helped writing resumes and directed them to interesting books.

The pool room had the worst table I'd ever played on. It was nowhere near level. Five of the banks were dead, it had three sweet spots on the rails. The cue sticks were warped beyond belief. After a week learning the terrible table, using my skills learned shooting snooker I could beat anyone there. Mostly I just shot my B or C game never using my A game unless someone started showing off. The blacks all had nicknames. A small guy they called Dipstick said he was a sous-chef. Mouseface, Jaybird, Nickleye, Cheesecutter, Smoothman, and Loveboat, all teased Dipstick, saying he got his name from falling out of his mama's ass all oily. They called me Slugger after I had my run in with Underwear Boy the dickless wonder.

When we'd take our piss tests, we'd be on video and watched by an orderly, to prevent all the scams invented. This lady with a Moe Howard haircut always seemed to be smiling at my One Eyed Willie, she sort of made me nervous. All of the ex-soldiers shared rooms and most nights I'd get up with a raging piss hard on, we were on closed circuit monitor and she'd hurry and spotlight my erection with her flashlight. I wasn't thinking about sex,

I just needed to pee. I'm pretty sure she had something else in mind.

I made it through the program and got most of my life back together. I've been sober over nine years, I keep my life simple and don't take anything for granted. For that melt down to happen at the age of fifty, is indescribable. People blame hording, murder, rape, incest, and all forms of insanity on being bipolar with severe panic attacks, it seems like it's the popular disease now in fashion.

I popped pills and did every drug there was and drank like a fish most of my life. I wrecked every car I'd ever owned for thirty five years. I don't know if the acid, weed, cocaine, heroin, glue, cough syrup, peyote, and mushrooms robbed me of my brain cells. I make no excuses for all the self-medicating I did. That's just a fancy expression for liking to be wasted. Now I walk a razorblade and ask for God's, my family, and your forgiveness.

In the long run, it doesn't matter what you do. Pray, make amends, stop alcohol and drugs, always tell the truth, and be honest with you or me. When you try to explain your mental disease, people won't understand unless they've walked in your shoes.

When you try suicide three times to escape your life like a coward and tell lots of lies, nobody will give a damn. No matter what, until you die, people won't forgive you or forget. All they will remember is you were a big liar and hurt their feelings. Even when you know you are closer to death than life and you no longer care what you own or owe and in your own mind you feel invincible. You will always be a pig wearing lipstick.

Water

The old man approached eighty years with no trepidation. The shadows crept closer challenging the sun. Death was a black widow slinking across its web. Getting into an ancient whaling boat, he pointed the prow west. The oars fit his hands like a woman. As land disappeared, icebergs with seals catching fish and polar bears catching seals floated by. He paid no attention, concentrating on the foggy horizon.

The farther the watery path took him the stronger he felt. Gnawing on dried blubber, he tossed chunks to passing seagulls. The sun and wind furrows that plowed his face and surrounded his
eyes vanished. His vision became clear and strong. Muscles in his arms, legs, and back bulged with an energy almost forgotten. Where land had once bridged a massive migration only the sea existed. Fifty seven miles across the Bering Sea passed in the blink of an eye.

Years dropped from the man like layers of skin on an onion. As he reached the tundra laden shore, his language had been left behind with his old body. A young man leaped from the boat. A red wine strength throbbed throughout him. His journey beckoned him south and west. For many miles he saw nothing. Then he noticed the tracks of wolves, he was no longer alone and yet he felt no fear. Cracking ice from a pond he drank deeply. That night sleeping under a billion diamonds, he knew it would be his last as a man. The wolves' content on an easy breakfast bounded down onto the man. His transformation into a caribou took less than a second. Striking out with sharp hooves, it sent several wolves tumbling and howling in pain. The caribou floated up from the ground and flew faster than lightning. It looked down at villages and rivers blurring below.

The snow topped mountains grew up from the earth toward heaven. A cold rain fell into an orange azure turquoise painted stream. A monolithic temple loomed above everything. Monks in saffron colored robes followed each other in solemn order. Workers drove herds of yaks and goats; some carried woven baskets of fish and cackling poultry. Others bore large bundles of wood tied together on their backs. The caribou de-incarnated into a hummingbird and watched the scenes from above. It was tiny enough to escape scrutiny. Flying into an open window in the temple, it followed more steps on its preordained path.

On an exquisitely carved jade pedestal a golden aura emanated. A gaunt parchment skinned monk opened the ruby and emerald encrusted amphora that exuded almost blinding light. It contained three hairs from Buddha. The hummingbird reached its final metamorphosis: a perfect snowflake. It floated down gently from above and settled glistening on the hairs of Buddha and melted

Mermaids and Gila Monsters

Standing in line at the grocery store with a quart of malt liquor, three lemons, and a liter of vodka; I ponder my future state of inebriation. The nightly escape a welcome companion, since my fourth wife ran away with a spoon. A lady in front of me has a package of super absorbent sanitary napkins, a ten pack of weenies, seven bananas, and some ginseng root. An old man behind me wears a gray immaculate wool coat and blue beret set at a jaunty angle, he must be at least seventy years old. He has a Penthouse, a Playboy, a Hustler, and a watermelon in his basket. Other than the checker the store seems empty. A dude enters in a black cape, black gaucho hat with dingle balls, a black raccoon eye mask, a can of cherry red paint in one hand, and a chrome hand cannon in the other. He sprays a huge Z on the screaming checker's apron, reaches into the cash register and grabs all the bills he can. The lady, the old man, and I dropped to the floor. I crack the seal on the vodka and take a stiff one. Tilting the bottle to the lady, she declines at first, the old man hits it like a bugle. Hearing the unmistakable sound of a shotgun shell being jacked into the chamber, we watch in astonishment as the checker blasts away at the retreating paint can marauder. His ass erupts in blood, meat, and gristle, as the buckshot tears into him. Sirens and nightingales sing in the gun smoke dusk, as I cup the lady's breast and chase the vodka with Colt 45. The old timer watches and cuts a round hole in his melon. The checker's face is smeared with a lunatic grin. I walk west toward the ocean swallowing the sun. The lady wrote her phone number on my chest in lipstick with a Z on my stomach. While mermaids and Gila monsters frolic in the persimmon sunset.

Picasso Left with Elvis

Pablito never cared much for eating pussy, saying it was like eating tuna through a picket fence. He complained of chapped lips, tired tongue, lock jaw, bushy eyebrows and mustache, and stretched out ears like tortillas. All Pablo craved was the missionary position with an occasional back door approach, but alas his reputation as a cunt gobbler preceded him. I told him repeatedly that he was the junkyard dog of poontang. He'd tilt his head back, grin and howl like a werewolf with hemorrhoids, revealing pubic hair caught between his teeth. "I need to get out of this hole I've dug." "Why don't you try bullfighting or spelunking or ornithology or become a Caliban?" I suggested. He packed a bag, got his record albums, and boogied. The doorbell rang, it was a dishwater blonde in a tight canary yellow dress, polka dot stiletto hills, and French fish net stockings. I rotated my neck muscles, stretched my tongue Komodo dragon fashion, and opened the door. The last vestiges of the sun were a dropping guillotine and an evil pumpkin moon was sneering down.

A Dirt Nap

Vladimir sat on the toilet and took care of his important business, upon finishing he found no paper. He yelled, "Natasha, you are a serial ass wiper." He spotted her special towel from Fragonard Parfumeur from France, taking his pocket knife out, he cut off a large piece. She must have figured out what he was up to. A fireman's axe came chopping through the flimsy door. Vladimir got up quick, but not fast enough to avoid the bowling ball. It knocked hit him into the bathtub and hit him in the face and head repeatedly. All he saw was indigo blue, apricot, bruise purple, and never come back black.

Peanut Dreams

First time a New Yorker moved to my hometown of Clovis, New Mexico and enrolled in my bricklaying class, I helped him and his lady find a place. It was a small trailer house on the edge of town. I noticed something through the kitchen window and went outside, there was a monster marijuana plant duct taped over the roof of the trailer. It took two of us to pull it by the roots. We chopped it into smaller pieces and hung it to dry. Jose the dude from the Big Apple was impressed, he pulled out a bag of primo smoke and we did some bongs and went and bought a case of Coors. I pulled out a bag of salted in the shell peanuts, he looked at me like I had leprosy and he explained about his allergy to them. I told him peanuts grow all around Clovis. Jose said it would be like being bit by a rattlesnake for him to eat one. I thought it a bit of an exaggeration. That night I made it home and dreamed about aliens, but instead of landing in Roswell, they landed in a peanut field. The aliens made Jose gorge on goobers, his body started inflating like a blimp and soon he was floating away over the horizon. I woke up and I was in bed with his woman. She didn't appear happy.

Hombre Lobo

"Hey dude, you're looking a shade ragged, for a hairy motherfucker." "Yea, I haven't been able to shit for three days, last full moon I got whacked out and ate a Mexican wino. He must have been full of cheese and beans and Mad Dog 20-20, I've been stopped up every since. Mind if I use your facilities?" "No problema amigo, but I have to warn you I've been meaning to move the outhouse and I never got around to it." Hombre Lobo took the trail down to the shit house. It was a gray wooden shack with a half moon cut in the door. When he got near, his canine nostrils flared and twitched in disgust. Hmmm he thought, smells like a combo of dead road kill skunk, stinky whore pinoche, and rotting barf. His belly was grumbling like a dump truck full of skeletons on a bumpy road. Fuck he thought stench and all. Opening the door, green bubble-eyed flies were playing soccer with a rat turd on the seat, a blood red spider with a hard on was waiting in its web for a snack. Lobo shooed them out and dropped his laundry. Just as his hairy ass cheeks hit wood, he heard muffled Chinese coming from between his legs. He rose up and peered down into the hole, two oriental men knee deep in shit were pushing a wheelbarrow. Too late the big one was on its way, Hombre Lobo let out a howl as he dropped the mother lode. The China men were cursing him. "Chinga, chow, chui, chop suey, you big hairy cocksucker shit machine." Just for that Lobo took a king sized wolf piss to wash them off. He walked back to the house and told his amigo what happened. "I forgot to tell you my neighbors wanted to fertilize their garden. Don't sweat it Lobo, you're the reason God made a middle finger."

Too Much Tabasco

Every Sunday Lawrence read the obituaries, first he read the names for people he might've known. Then he looked at photos and ages, for people younger than him. His mortality struck him as humorous in his own befuddled state of queerness. One morning after coffee and a breakfast burrito, Lawrence opened the paper to the obits and there bigger than Dallas was a photo of himself. Before he could focus, a smoke belching chainsaw ground through the paper into his face. Eyeballs squirted from his head, hair and grayish brain matter splashed and splattered the ceiling and his Lazy Boy. His new boyfriend cleaned up the mess and made a pitcher of Bloody Larry's and sat back and watched an Alfred Hitchcock movie.

Phuque Book

Xavier was considered a geek by most. He preferred it that way, while laughing all the way to the bank. Ninety percent of the adult population had purchased one of his inventions at one time or another. Xavier liked to fly under the radar. He made Frosty the Snowman look like the devil in a blue dress with alligator sneakers. In gas stations, truck stops, bars, taverns, and cantinas his inventions were dispensed from vending machines. At grocery and drug stores his products were sold in larger quantities. His first invention was called, Instant Pussy (a small foam foldable cat in a condom like wrapper), it was nothing more than a cheap gimmick. Later he discovered a way to insert a masturbation hole & doubled the price. The new and improved Instant Pussy was a huge hit. X's second big seller was flavored ribbed condoms; chocolate cherry, vanilla cinnamon, bacon and lettuce, garlic pickle, fried chicken, buttered popcorn, and pepperoni pizza. He kept surprising the public with more far out flavors. Soon he had more money than he could spend in many lifetimes. Then he watched the movie about the creator of face book, his mind exploded with an idea. Xavier could not sleep, he paced like a captured Bengal tiger, his mind on fire with creativity. He hired the three top experts in the world of computer technology, providing them with equipment and a state of the art laboratory. For six months they slaved over equations and conquered all seemingly insurmountable odds. Finally they were successful in creating the most fantastic voyage of mankind: PHUQUE BOOK. Anyone anywhere in the world could have safe sex with anyone else, for a nominal fee of course. Xavier cut each of the three experts in for a percentage of the profits. He kept the lion's share, married a lady from Mozambique, bought an island and was almost never heard from again. He came forward only once more to receive his Nobel piece prize and donate his entire fortune to the NAACP.

A Coma in Oklahoma

She pulled off her chartreuse crotch less panties with a striptease flair. I was harder than the howitzer cannons I fired during my stint in the army. Her almost hairless almond pussy reminded me of a baby sheep's mouth as she danced and swirled around the room. The news had an important breaking story on television. I craned my neck to see what was happening, but all I saw was her bra flying onto a fake Picasso painting and bouncing into the aquarium. I pinned her tight firm body to the couch and started pumping granite. She farted, squealed, screeched, quivered, finally sounded like a fog horn in Maine, I ripped her spider web lace nylons from her smooth legs and shoved them down her throat. I never noticed her becoming limp as a strand of spaghetti. After I finished I threw her body in a dumpster, pissed, and fired up a cigar. Then I watched Walter Cronkite talk about a bomb blowing up a government building, a commercial about douche bags and peanut butter.

Going Postal

After 34 years in a Kafkaesque dream in a big ugly concrete seagull dropping covered building, I was finally able to say adios. The main post office in Milwaukee was open 24 hours a day, every day of the year. When Jeffrey Dahmer was captured, it seemed like a new game was invented: Blow Up the Cannibal. We were evacuating every other day, it was a nice in a weird way, kind of like sex with an alien. In December, twelve hour overtime was mandatory the entire month because of the Christmas rush. When you least expected it, you could find yourself elbow to elbow with people covered in cat hair, bad garlic breathers, flatulent bags, phlegm cougher, perfume nose rapists, and booger pickers all sorting letters to Santa. People came, not because they liked it, but food was a motivator. The work was boring and tedious, until the ricin letter bombs to Washington, D.C. The letter sorting machines would grab an envelope with dried rice and talcum powder & spray a huge area. Hazmat teams would walk around in space suits, sometimes with dogs. I thought of the poor canines as canaries in a coal mine. The bosses were trained in the Adolf Hitler School of supervision. This guaranteed low production and dissension in the ranks. Day after day folks trudged into the building like lobotomized robots, being slowly ground into pencil shavings and ash. The seniority system ruled; new blood on nights, juniors on afternoons, and old timers on days. After years of sucking manure through a straw, you finally got to sleep like a human, but forget weekends off, that comes when you are ready to retire or die. Needless to say you are stuck with the same old faces your entire career. The men get beer bellies, hair falling out, and teeth getting loose. Women getting fat, neck and face turning prune like, time swallowing their beauty. Workers becoming family, loving each other or hating and backstabbing as the situation calls for. Violence not uncommon, weapons concealed in abundance. Management dictating from their side of the fence, with bullet proof vests and stupid smirks trying to epitomize vicious threats. Many play hide the salami, leapfrog in the dark, smoke grass while reading the Bible in their cars. Always feeling tempted to walk away or doing the defecation diarrhea disco all over where you earn, it is usually never worth it. On the other hand you can't take it with you.

Nestled In the Paloverde

The lemon yellow sun dribbled day light juice onto the elephant colored rails. Taking out my last cigar, I watched the sun die. Reaching into my pocket I felt two quarters squirming, my guts were growling like a wolf man eating a vampire. I entered the hobo camp smelling food beckoning my quivering taste buds. I saw men with brown bags, holding strong fortified vino. Laying my money and stogie next to the campfire, a man dished me up a plate. Saluting him and smiling my thanks, I knew I'd have to find work, but for now one thing was certain, someone sure could cook. After meeting up with my Pueblo amigo, Puma and building a fireplace in Espanola, New Mexico, I felt restless. I suggested a trip to New Orleans. Puma had never seen the Mississippi and I wanted to consult with a voodoo woman, I'd heard about. Walking down Bourbon Street, listening to Dixieland jazz and blues, once in awhile we would start dancing. Musicians and tourists gawked and grinned. Puma borrowed a guitar and I sang some songs in Spanish and recited a few poems. An old man jumped off his porch and played congas, flute, and harmonica. Several coins and bills were deposited into the gent's sombrero. He fed us hot gumbo and crawdads and we drank chicory coffee laced with hooch. The house of the voodoo woman was in an alley near the river. Puma recognized most of the herbs hanging from her ceiling beams. There were jars of chicken and goat feet and eyeballs of all sizes and pungent repugnant odors. I asked for a cure for baldness, she mixed several ingredients and took it behind a curtain for a minute. When she returned, she instructed me to stir it well before drinking. Once you return home, she said use your own warmed urine. Puma was trying to keep a straight face. When we got back to the mountains, I decided I wasn't cooking any piss and I damn sure wasn't drinking it. Puma and I drank the datura tea, near the Painted Desert. Flocks of ravens perched on azure rocks pecking slowly at purple lizards. Stag horn cholla, agave stars, and barrel cacti leaned west toward the sun and Pacific. A turtle dove nestled in the paloverde. Puma pointed at a red rattler swallowing a kangaroo mouse. Clouds exploded in crimson, green, yellow, orange, intaglio; surrealistic bleeding hallucinations. Overpowered and frightened, we drank mescal until oblivion accepted us. The next day we boarded a freight train south for Oaxaca and the pyramids. Near the zocalo in Mexico City, I went to buy blue agave tequila. An old woman called to me, I reached for a few pesos. As I put the coins in her hand, she held onto mine and rubbed it with red powder. Her voice took on an unearthly quality. I felt dizzy and my legs were watery. The day became dark; the sun was swallowed by evil thunderheads. She spoke in what sounded like German. "You will live a few more years, and then die like a dog." She wanted more money, I staggered away, feeling a terrible need to be scratched behind my ears.

Hiding in My Wounds

While raking leaves of golden red, my typing machine gun flies out the window smashing on the sidewalk next to me, scattering into the street. I figured it was coming and overdue, after all the fights about my writing and priorities. Twenty years of putting words on paper, trees had it better. So did whores and airplane pilots and clouds and frogs. Thirty years in the post office helped give me the nervous mental breakdown and stroke, shakes, and froze the left side of my body, so I spoke like a gangster. I had a ratty desk I picked up off the street on the way home from my first visit to the nuthouse and that was where I attempted to create. On my second visit to the land of loonies I was put in group with five women and one man, that had punched out a guy with a bowling pin while buying a lemon Ford pickup, he taught me how to watch television, a skill I had all but forgotten. One young chick had kept her car running in closed garage. One hefty mama from Canada liked dogs a bit too much. A black lady was trembling like a mean dog with a jalapeno shoved up its rectum. The other two thought they were vampires, their necks were covered in hickies. Our session just got underway when it felt like the earth had been raped. We were in a hospital next to Lake Michigan and a Russian ship had smashed into it. Dr. Jado did number one and two in her panties. She was a pill pushing pretender of a shrink and thought Buddha was just another name for booty call. She was about to kick me out of her group because I let her know when she was wrong. Dr. Jado had a pill for everything, instead of acupuncture, therapy, or hypnotism. If you were shooting sparks out your behind, she would find a pill. I was finally given the boot. When I got home it was my daughter's birthday, I shaved my moustache. My wife had never seen me stash less. I guess my snow white lip scared her, it resembled an albino caterpillar. I crashed in the basement again, I had my army mummy bag. Concrete never gets softer, but there's a roof and walls.

How I Pulled the Rabbit Out of the Hat

Paco's father was the finest jeweler in Santa Fe, he passed down his skill. Paco could make anything. He preferred silver, turquoise, coral, and bear claws, but would sometimes work with gold and precious gems. Paco's thirst was unquenchable, he'd drink anything at anytime, anywhere.

How he became a boss on a surveying crew for the Santa Fe National Forest Service was unfathomable to me. He spoke mostly Spanglish and was out of shape because of his constant drinking. Surveying timber roads up mountainsides isn't for sissies. Paco would sweat rivers of eighty proof and pour more booze down his throat at every stop.

One Friday night he asked if I was going to Albuquerque. I replied yes. He asked me to sell some jewelry for him. I thought about it, I'd made one successful selling trip to Milwaukee, so I agreed. He loaded up a jewelry case and put in a snub nose pistol in case of trouble. I drove south the seventy miles, past the penitentiary, across the Pueblo land of red hills, yuccas, and tumble weeds.

Old Town was packed with tourists, the plaza swarming. I gave a Navajo elder fifty bucks to share a corner of his blanket. I was hotter than a July jalapeno, doing almost four grand in business by early afternoon. I never noticed three pachucos giving me the eye. At dusk I made for the cantina overlooking the trickling Rio Grande. After a good meal of enchiladas and sopapillas washed down with several ice cold Tecates with lime and coarse salt, I felt great. I saw a phone booth in the parking lot and decided to share my good news with Paco.

"Hey amigo, I kicked ass and took names today. Seven grand and I still have a third of the merchandise." I heard a tapping on the glass behind me. "Hold on a minute, Paco." I turned around and saw three pistols and a sawed off shotgun all aimed at my chest by four greasy looking low riders. The leader had buck teeth and a steel marble eyeball. "Holy hell, Paco, I'm being robbed."

"Robbed? Robbed? That's my stuff, you gringo weasel. You're making theese sheet up," he yelled, cursing me in Spanglish. The phone booth door opened, I was facing four cases of lead poison.

"Give us your money and trinkets and we might let you live." I could hear Paco screaming in the background, "They're bluffing, don give theem jacksheet." Handing over the goods, the hoods drove off. Paco was still screaming as I hung up. That night I crashed at a friend's. At noon the next day I drove to Paco's, his wife, Ramona answered the door. "Were you really robbed?" she asked. I nodded. "Paco is pissed." I nodded again.

"You were supposed to go to Rabbit Mountain this morning. They waited as long as they could."

"Maybe we can get through by radio relay from the ranger's station?"

Thirty minutes later, Paco is cursing me and my ancestors. "You cost me ten grand and now you're probably screwing my wife." "I'm on my way." When I arrived he was pacing the forest service cabin, a bottle of tequila almost empty. "You lying piece of crap," he bellowed grabbing my shirt. I kneed his nuts, he puked for a while. Some guys helped me clean him up and stick him in his bunk. The next morning I woke up and was staring into his blood red eyes. "You got any money?" he asked.

"Nope," I replied. I had four c-notes stashed in my boot. "Then you are going to be my gringo slave. Remember that fireplace we talked about? That's just for starters. I want a circular bull's eye window over my front door and an arch going into the backyard, all made out of iron pyrite. We can haul that fool's gold out of the old silver mines in Tijeras Canyon." I thought fool's gold, how appropriate. "Every waking hour we're not surveying or fighting fire, you belong to me."

I used all my talents with a trowel that my family taught me. We heaved the stones into a bucket and winch set up over a four month period, I completed all the work. I had never worked so hard or been that long without a woman. Ramona was a big woman, Rubenesque and intelligent. She could really rustle up the grub and had an inviting smile. Paco didn't appreciate what he had. He'd bring his drunken amigos over to show them his white slave and the work being done. He'd get this dreamy look in his glazed bloodshot eyes. The last checks from the forest service came before winter set in and we faced a four month lay-off. I gave Paco six hundred of my money and said we were even. "I still theenk you rip me off."

I looked at my calloused hands, his stone wall fireplace with Mexican marble hearth, the perfectly chiseled window, and arch. Gathering my tools, I could see Ramona's sadness. I said, "Paco, I'm sorry I lost your stuff, but you got the better end of this bargain." Just as I pulled out of their driveway, I saw the leader of the gang that robbed me. The sun glistened off that unforgettable eye, he had the case they'd taken from me under his arm. I waited a few hours and called Ramona, to ask about the situation. When she heard my description of the leader, she said it was Paco's first cousin and I had been scammed. I asked her if she wanted to leave Paco and head south for a warmer climate. She agreed at once.

We've been in Guaymas on the Sea of Cortez for ten years. Ramona brought a king's ransom in jewels. I fish and we garden and grow yerba buena. Our rabbits take lessons from us.

Bring Me an Apple with No Worms

After attending a brief writer's workshop and reading and presenting several stories and poems, I got a letter from the cute female instructor. "I feel there is something lurking deeper behind your words than fornication, defecation, and masturbation. The class is quite taken with you. The plump young lady that writes about her chiropractor performing the Harley-Davidson kick start maneuver on her sacroiliac is obsessed with you. The old grandma that keeps bringing you vagina shaped cookies is crazy for you. The gay guy can't remove his eyes from your well-endowed crotch. You have blown my mind with your work and persona. I wake up at night and have to reach for Mr. Buzzy while fantasizing about you. The community center has agreed to fund an anthology of our collective writing. Would you agree to be editor?" I wrote back in the affirmative with a dinner invitation. One thing leads to another, happily I might add. Later I submitted some poems about me having sex with gay zombie dogs; I felt I wasn't the proper judge of my own work.

Mamasita Mambo

Her bush felt like a Brillo pad, all trimmed for exotic dancing. She undressed him and mounted. She started riding like the Texas Rangers were in hot pursuit and she'd be free if she could cross the Rio Grande. They fucked and sucked in almost every conceivable position. Resting between orgasms for wine, finally he split. The azure sky was filled with purple bruised fingers groping the sun. He staggered like a punch drunk boxer back into the day. The sunlight hit his eyes like a cop's interrogation torture lamp. His head throbbed and his tongue felt like it was growing green bologna fur fungus. As he took a breath of fresh air, a Santa Fe Chief locomotive blew by screaming its whistle. Feeling like he'd passed out in some alley with his mouth open and a wino had taken a piss in it for a cheap laugh, he finally got his brain strain together so he could grab a couple of cups of java and some greasy eggs. Going to the bank seemed like a brilliant idea. The woman appeared to be in her late forties, a little over the hill, but extremely well taken care of. If she'd dye her hair it would take at least 5 years off her appearance. She led Nicky into the vault. As she placed her key next to his, her breasts brushed up against his hand. This sent a tingle through them both. The lady looked him in the eyes and sucked in her breath. Nicky gave her his best smile, as she led him to a private cubicle. She opened the door and he entered with his metal box. He pulled her in behind him, the box forgotten. She started to protest, but Nicky was kissing her full and deep. Any questions about what was about to happen disappeared as he cupped and massaged her fine ass through her silky dress, pulling her to him. She moaned as he pulled her panties to the side and with a feather like stroke erected her juicy clitoris and nibbled at her hardening nipples through the fabric. He guided her down onto the thick plush carpet and ripped off her lacy white panties. They split at the seams; they were beyond caring. With her dress around her hips,

Nicky let his tongue do its magic. The lady groaned and tugged at his belt and unzipped his fly and freed his stiff boner. Placing soft wet hungry kisses up and down his dick and then sucking greedily at the tip, she knew her business. Almost beyond ready, he mounted and worked fast, banging her head against the flimsy wooden wall of the cubicle. The harder he thrust, the more she liked it. She was so vocal, he stuffed her mouth with her shredded panties. They climaxed together. Wiping off, he checked his box. While she wiped hers and put herself back together. Mercedes had beaten him to the safety deposit box. Every person in the bank watched as they exited the vault area. Nicky waited for a standing ovation. The lady blushed right down to where her panties should have been. He made a quick survey of the women, always checking for future fornication prospects. Nicky walked out of the bank, headed west and north.

Jackalope Condoms

I shook hands with Leo. His dreadlocks almost put my eye out when he turned his head. Standing next to their tour bus, I admired Bob Marley's stoned to the bone likeness. I wiped the marijuana and patchouli off my hand onto my blue jeans. I asked him in Spanish if he spoke English.

"Most assuredly, amigo," he replied with a heavy accent.

"Do you cats have any spleef?" I asked.

"Hell yes, gringo. Let's go to the room."

We were staying in the same hotel in Guadalajara. His room held three Rasta dudes from Chile and two yaga men from Oaxaca. The room was filled with swirling smoke. Six young fine mamacitas were dancing and stripping. There were mushrooms and peyote and big piles of grass on every surface. I hadn't seen so much dope since a Hendrix concert in Albuquerque and I worked back stage.

Two amigos were playing Santana, two were playing jungle drum riffs from what sounded like Ginger Baker's Cream solos. The party was turning into a frenzy, like a nest of cobras mangling and making love to a cage of hungry tigers.

I whipped out a chapbook and started reading a poem. The best looking of the babes ripped off her bra and panties and started unzipping my fly. I tried to finish my poem, to the wild applause of the room full of musicians. She took me to the bathroom and we did it standing up against the sink.

Later we jammed into the mezcalito night. Leo hired me to open for them the next night. He said the gig paid $50, which was more than most poetry paid. I had to read earlier at the Gandhi Bookstore. It was a good thirty minute read, I sold eight books. The owner insisted we play hide the tamale before I could split. She reminded me of Sophia Loren.

I met the men from Chile on Calzada Indepencia in front of a large auditorium. We did damage to several blunts before I took my white butt out on stage. I read and chugged wine from a goat skin. Three women climbed on stage and handed me money and phone numbers. I think they wanted me to wail, get off or ball their brains out after the party.

Leo and One Love hit their mark, loud and impressive. I'd never seen Marley, but these motherhumpers cooked and sizzled. The joint was jumping, but I was craving some air. They owed me $50, but money is an iguana eating a jackalope. I headed for the capital and clean threads and a much needed bath.

After three days in Mexico City with a new lady friend, exploring Frida Kahlo's Casa Azul, Trotsky's fort like house, museums, and our hotel pool, Leo called from Santiago. He said the condors above Machu Picchu were disappearing.

"Can you come down and do a condor benefit read?"

I explained the situation to my lady. She shrugged.

"Let's do it," I replied.

"Bring some condoms, at least four hundred," Leo said.

"Why?"

"You'll find out," he chuckled.

I didn't know whether we were going to copulate with gigantic birds or Incans. I purchased the French envelopes and boarded the next flight. The plane took off and a natural blonde stewardess rubbed her breasts on my face. I thought, looks like there might be a few missing rubbers by the time I get to Chile. Her cascading hair had an angel like quality with the sunlight shining through it.

I forgot to ask Leo the Rastafarian how much I was getting paid. Who cares? I'm eight miles high and I just got a pair of perfumed panties served with my golden agave juice.

A Geronimo Moon

Maybe it was thoughts about Geronimo or the brick smokestack jutting up against the dark Milwaukee night that made me think about the lean times when I was a kid back in New Mexico. I stood outside my parent's bedroom door and could hear them talking about money, how we'd be lucky to have enough food for the family through winter. My dad said he'd take me and we'd go to California to work in an asbestos factory. A bricklayer friend of his had called the week before telling him about the job.
"It's easy money. You sit around playing cards on the clock until the asbestos gets too hot and blows out a wall. Then you put on a protective suit and go in the foundry and rebuild the wall. It's all glazed eight inch block, level work. No speed leads, nothing fancy," my dad explained.

My mother begged him not to take me. Saying I was too young and my lungs could be damaged.

"Look honey, we're up against a hard place. I need my son. He's a good hand and we have no choice." I could tell by his voice, he was none too happy with the situation.

"Just be careful and call when you get there," my mother said.

"We will and try not to worry. Get your gear together, son, we need to get on the payroll."

I packed clothes, tools, a book of poetry by Pablo Neruda, and a book about Apaches. Our red pickup muscled south, through the sage brush and tumbleweeds. I loved the country we were traveling through. Peanut and soybean farms, cattle ranches sprouted up like goat head weeds through the asphalt. Windmills pumped water from deep underground so man and beast could survive.

We listened to the radio for weather forecasts. Soon we topped a rise and could see Roswell. We bought coffee and tamales there and headed for Alamogordo. We crossed the White Sands, where scientists had exploded the first nuclear bomb.

"You feel anything, dad?" I asked.

"What do you mean, son?"

"Radiation, do you feel it?" I asked.

"We've got more important business," he answered.

He put the hammer down on the old red truck. The road and tires whined and protested like an old anarchist. Near Las Cruces, we crossed the Camino Real; looking up we could see the cross lit up against the blue hills. I tried to imagine Coronado and his conquistadors looking for The Seven Cities of Gold. The radio was picking up mariachi music from Juarez. My dad sang along. His Spanish was better than mine.

We bore due west along the bottom of the state. My dad told me about Geronimo and Pancho Villa's daring raid into the United States. We made a fast detour south of Deming to see the state park dedicated to Villa. The thick walled adobe contained photos of Zapata and Villa and many weapons of Mexican and American soldiers from that time. Sombreros, swords, bullets, and arrows were all mounted on display. The building was surrounded by a garden of desert cacti; cat's claw with tiny red berries, yucca, Joshua trees, agave, and fragrant mesquite.

The desert was deceptively quiet as we passed through Lordsburg. A dust storm obliterated the line between New Mexico and Arizona. Outside of Tucson, we finally took a rest. We pulled into a motel, like nothing I had ever seen before. Each room was a concrete teepee. Our beds were close together and you could barely squeeze into the bathroom. There was no swimming pool. The stars and moon were beautiful, so I didn't watch the tiny television in our room. My dad was sawing logs before me.

During the night something felt odd. I thought it was thirst or being in a strange setting. I was too tired to get up and check it out. The next morning I woke up and was surprised to see my dad wasn't up. He always got up before me.

I looked over toward his bed and saw something brown and thick. It looked like oil. Pulling back the sheets, I saw an arrow protruding from my dad's chest. His eyes were open staring up at me. Blood was everywhere. The arrow looked like it was Chiricahua Apache. I felt myself sinking to my knees. I was dizzy and nauseated. I held on to my sanity and ran to the office.

We called the police. The cops came and put me in their car and took me to the station. One officer brought me coffee. My hands were shaking so bad I spilled it all over. He wiped it up and later he brought me a soda and a sandwich. A lady came and questioned me. She was very understanding. She let me call home, once I settled down a bit.

My mother answered and I told her about dad. She became hysterical and started screaming. I heard a loud noise as the phone receiver bounced on the kitchen floor. I could hear my older sister trying to find out what had happened and at the same time calm my mother. The lady that questioned me spoke to my sister. After several hours we both spoke to my mother. They kept me in a room all day while they investigated. I read my book about Apaches. I studied the names of Geronimo's eight wives: Alope, Chee-hash-kish, Nana-tha-thtith, Zi-yeh, She-gha, Shtsha-she,

Ihtedda, and Azul. Finally a man in a suit came in and said I was being released. He told me I could go.

I called home and my sister answered the phone.

"I know you've been through a lot. We can take care of the funeral arrangements. I know you're young and I wouldn't blame you if you came home, right now. With dad gone, you are the man of the house. We still need money, worse than ever now. You decide what you must do," my sister told me.

I got in the old red truck and pointed it toward the land where oranges come from. I concentrated on the yellow line on the highway. All I could see was my dad's staring eyes.

Next Time

I checked my grenades, my stiletto, and my .357. The liquor store was about to close. The fucking sign had driven me insane. The Coldest Beer in Milwaukee, like they actually knew that for a fact. There was a Mexican whore with a parrot sitting on her shoulder paying for a pint of Old Granddad. The bird was giving me the mean eye actually, they both were. I pulled out my pistol and my dick. I bitch-slapped the Arab owner between the eyes, knocking his funky ass turban off. Blood dribbled over his name tag, which read Kelly. His real name was Kolbir and he hated Americans. Fucking Arabs should never fuck with the Irish. I wanted some action from the whore but the fucking parrot flew down and landed on my Johnson. It was stiletto and Thanksgiving time for the birdie. There was another woman in the store. She was blonde and wearing a suit and carrying an alligator briefcase. Her body was hidden, but well endowed. I motioned her over near the cash register. She took a package of lubricated cinnamon condoms from her case. This babe was ready. I took the blonde standing up and then she sucked and sucked, until I felt myself exploding and I put the .357 in her ear and pulled the trigger. Her brains splattered all over my nuts. I drank half a bottle of tequila, then had the Mexican wash me. Her pussy farted as I fucked her in the wine aisle. She kicked and broke seven bottles of burgundy as I rammed it up her tight frijoles packed ass. She pleaded and sucked hard as I slipped the stiletto between her ribs. I called Jesus. We carted out all the liquor and the bodies. Jesus got his jollies with the Arab. The money was piss poor. Next time, I hope the beer is colder. I don't want to sue for false advertising.

The Trade

The pit bulls jaws clamped down on her leg before I knew what happened. The dog had come flying out of nowhere. My daughter was screaming as I clawed at the dog's throat and gouged its eyes. I strained against its neck muscles to no avail. Reaching inside its jaws, I wrenched some relief for my little girl. My fingers were being sawed to the bone. My wife came running from the house with my big Bowie knife I used for deer hunting. The knife was heavy and razor sharp. I hacked once, twice, sawing the dog's head off. The dog's jaw muscles finally relaxed their grip. My daughter had passed out from the shock. My wife cradled her head as I examined her wound. It didn't look too bad, it was in the fleshy part of her thigh. Then I noticed my hands were bleeding badly. Two fingers were missing from my right hand, the left was minus a pinky. Ripping my shirt I made bandages for my daughter and myself. I looked at the dog's head, there hanging out of its mouth were what was left of my fingers. One glassy eye seemed to stare at me in triumph. I gave the head a good kick, I knew I'd made a good bargain. My wife ran after it to retrieve my fingers. A garbage truck came around the corner, squashing the dog's brains all to hell.

Soldier

A few stars hung overhead like nail holes in a black wall. Soldier looked up and continued walking at a brisk pace toward the barely discernable tracks. His part in the war was always following warily a few feet behind. He was once an elite shadow of a Long Range Reconnaissance Patrol.

Chained dogs roamed in the yards of slumbering humanity, growling at the gates of hell. He needed to fight again, to kill to prove himself worthy. Some nights in the waning darkness, Soldier would recall the adrenalin abyss whisper rush, orgasmic sweat soaking his body. Uncontrollable dreams of clean kills and remorselessness stirred an inferno in his loins. Looking around, Soldier saw graveyard emptiness; his heart leaped green mountains of verdure.

It had been over twenty five years since he last tasted the exhilaration of a human hunt. The evocation of his demons freed and condemned him at the same time. The tracks beckoned him. He carried his cross every time his eyelids closed, every step he took.

Soldier crawled through the underbrush into a distant time. He was miles into Laos, behind enemy lines. Ahead dressed in tan, the uniform of an officer, his target leaned against a thick stand of bamboo, weapon out of reach. Soldier's knife came alive in his fist. He became a dervish of death. Four humans lay staring in carnage at the jungle canopy with lifeless eyes. The stench of blood filled his nostrils, his mouth stretched in an unholy smile. There was no memory of the three men. The woman officer was like a horror movie, he saw his right hand yank her head back, his left draw the blade in an arc across her soft throat. Her head dangled from a flap, death gurgled crimson onto the jungle floor.

Her body slumped; her cap askew, long blue black hair blossomed free like a waterfall at midnight.

Soldier stood over her and studied her face. Even death could not remove or erase her beauty. Dark almond eyes stared at him questioningly, accusingly, his tortured soul screamed, he knelt beside her. In a different world he might have been a young man proposing marriage. He raised her tiny exquisite hands to his lips, tears spilled a turmoil of hate and love. Soldier heard voices.

"Hey mister, have you got a cigarette?" a girl asked.

He looked in the direction of the voice, he was back. Two lovely young ladies were looking at him inquisitively. Soldier offered them two of his smokes. They lit up, their lipstick bright on the filters.

"Some men are after us, can you help us? We need a place to hide."

He looked deep into their eyes. "Follow me. We'll take the side streets." One of them took his hand and rubbed it against her cheek. The other kissed him on the forehead. Soldier felt the taste of blood inside his mouth. He reached inside his jacket for his knife, where it had lain like a scar for too years.

Brujo

Puma's eyes narrowed to slits, his nostrils dilated like his namesake testing the air for danger. He disappeared into the chaparral, like a wild creature of the wind. The splashing might've been a grass carp or gar turning over in the water, but never leaving things to chance is how you remained alive. The tree frogs soon resumed their romantic croaking for a mate.

Puma slithered through the grama grass downstream before rising. I stayed between the horses and quietly snapped a clip into my lightning stick. Puma approached the fire stealthily, to warm his hands. Something was bothering him; I could see a smoldering anger, a bordering insecurity.

"What is it?" I whispered.

"Not sure."

A bullet tugged at his sleeve, burning a furrow up his arm. Another bullet blew the heel off his boot. His favorite horse was shot to pieces, heavy slugs made the animal jerk, as he used it for cover. An unearthly scream cackle echoed through the canyon. The heavy boom of Puma's buffalo rifle followed the muzzle flashes of the attackers. At a run, I fired bursts of M-16 tumblers. The canyon grew quiet. I guessed it was Puma's trouble, but it could as easily have been mine.

We scouted the barranca, finding the tracks of two men. We rousted a diamondback, a covey of quail, and a woodpecker. Puma had some tesquino corn beer. We built up the fire and filled our bed rolls with stones.

Taking the high ground, we drank and waited. The stars and clouds swam through the skies. The night was a brujo in disguise.

Tiger Skin Blues

Silvio walked through the park picking up dead squirrels he'd croaked with his pea shooter. He used voodoo to bring them back to life. Almost anything was possible when you were a sorcerer of his stature. One day, Silvio saw a woman with a knockout body and long lustrous red hair wearing a burgundy velvet turban. She was walking a regal full grown tiger on a leash with a diamond studded collar. The tiger's name was Antonio, hers was Cruz. They were intrigued by Silvio. He took off his magic hat and put a squirrel inside and the tiny animal jumped out, stood on its hind legs and chattered in Spanish plain as day. Cruz was amazed, Antonio was hungry. Cruz asked Silvio for a squirrel for her tiger. At first he refused. After much bargaining, they came to a mutual agreement. She would give Silvio a real good time for each squirrel. Antonio gobbled them down like jelly beans, much like the bullets that bounce off Superman's chest when villains shoot him. This went on satisfactorily for many years. Antonio grew fat and contented; their love prospered. One day, Silvio went shopping for oysters, clam chowder, zig-zags, beer nuts, bananas, and malt liquor. On his way home he was accosted by a group of squirrel lover advocates. They'd been watching Silvio for quite a while. They beat him within an inch of his life and left him in the park. A gang of tree rats finished him off. Cruz's heart was broken into a million pieces. Her tears could've filled the Gulf of Mexico. Antonio couldn't survive on ordinary cat food; he hit his eighth life quick. Cruz had him made into a rug and there she slept, until she died of boredom and a lonely heart.

Porcupine Ice Cream

The fat lady from a few doors down called, referring to her husband, "Dickless will be gone all day. Can I come visit, sweetie?" "Why not, make it quick though, I have yard work to do." This situation with Daisy had been going on a few months. She was a pretty woman and took care of herself, except she had a big fat bulging ass. She loved to have me spank it all pink and warm and kneed it like fresh dough, as I split her open like a pomegranate and fucked her silly. I was riding her elephant style, when her cell phone went off with music from The Adams Family and Lurch's voice saying, "You rang?"

"It's Tiny Scrotum, he's only a few blocks away on his way home, and I gotta go." I withdrew and gave her a pearl necklace all over her tits, mouth, and in her left eye. Looking over through the window I saw my neighbor next door. She looked like Martha Stewart and she was laughing, like one of her prison cronies had just finished a fresh batch of fermented bread and fruit toilet pruno and they'd been licking each other's clitorises. I pointed at my watch and shrugged my shoulders. I went to my garage and got out the lawn mower. There was this homely bum looking barfly chick eyeing a bag of cans, I always wondered what the difference was between homely and downright dog shit ugly.

She looked me over and said, "Hey mister, you want a good blowjob cheap?"

"I don't have much money."

"How much you got?"

I emptied my pockets. "I have three dollars and seventy four cents. You can have those cans and I have a new chapbook, I can give you."

"What's a chapbook?"

"Just some bullshit I write down and it gets stapled together into a little pamphlet. I write stuff like: Your tender lovely lips caressing my love organ of delight." I lowered my laundry and watched her expression.

She took one look and said, "Hell fire, if I knew you were packing that magnum and could talk like that, it would've been on the house with no negotiations." She could gobble goober with the best of them.

Later I waved across the street to the Sofia Vergara, only better lady. We were having an Oysters Rockefeller supper together, she came over for a quick tongue embracing kiss. Her tight purple shirt revealed her huge mouth-watering bouncing plum breasts, true buttery eggplant beauties. Her visiting cousin was dead ringer for the bombshell blonde, Kelly Ripa. She slipped me her phone number, after she ran her smooth hands up and down my inner thighs, then she backed her ass up to my face like a dump truck full of hundred dollar bills. The idea of doing the locomotion with that fine mojo almost broke me and stroked me. I needed a siesta, so I said adios muchachas.

Throwing Curve Balls

My son came home from school complaining of his new teacher. Him being an excellent student, it surprised me. My lady usually handled these affairs, but she happened to be busy that day, so I told my son to relax, that I could check into the matter.

It was late afternoon when I approached the school. The place seemed deserted, my footsteps echoed through the halls. My son had assured me his teacher always stayed late grading papers. I knocked at the door and heard a muffled voice, say come in. The woman was seated, but she appeared tall and thin and wore a well-tailored suit. She was attractive in a strange sort of way. I told her who I was and why I had come to see her. She pointed to a chair next to her desk and asked me to be seated.

I was completely and utterly shocked at what happened next. She smelled of roses, cinnamon, and hyacinth. Her voice was silky and husky as she whispered in my ear her intentions. I was totally shocked and captivated. Her lips were petulant soft velvet brushing their way down my body. Her strong yet delicate fingers lowered my zipper and reached inside. Getting down on her knees between my legs, she lowered my pants and shorts. She nuzzled my thighs and tongued the end of my erection. Cupping my balls and expertly sucking and licking the entire length of my scrotum, around and up and down ever so slowly.

I felt the tiny hairs on the nape of my neck stand up with electricity. At this maddening rate I wouldn't be able to hold back for long. I tried to think some dick wilting thoughts, to prolong the pleasure. She must've sensed this and when my mind strayed, she carefully gave me a few bites to bring me back to the business at hand.

I soon spurted my spunk into her greedy mouth. She pushed and massaged my balls inside me, to drain every drop in my body. She swallowed my load and gave me a big French kiss. I could have done without the kiss, but didn't want to offend her and ruin my son's scholastic record by protesting.

By this time, I wanted more than a blowjob. I picked her up and swiveled her up onto her desk, scattering papers everywhere. I crushed her lips with mine, drowning out her moans and pleas. As I reached into her panties, I was about to get my second surprise of the day. There taped down to her thigh was a boner almost as big as mine. Needless to say, I had found my dick wilting thoughts after all. I left the room under a vow of mutual silence and from that moment on my son's grades improved.

Defying Logic and Gravity

After an exhausting book festival with dismal sales, I fell asleep with Star Trek on. My two cats were speaking together in my dream.

"Look at that piss poor example of humanity."

One cat was flying near the ceiling doing figure eights and somersaults.

"Even if we let him choose, the ability to fly, defecate gold, or communicate with all creatures, he probably couldn't make up his mind."

The cat landed, grunted and a small turd of gold appeared. They called and ordered a pizza with extra anchovies. The doorbell soon rang and one cat flew up and unlocked the door. The note they had written lay in plain sight. It read I hope you accept gold instead of cash. The pizza man hefted the gold and bit down on it and smiled. The cats shut the door and laughed like crazy.

I woke up and both cats were passed out next to a stinky empty pizza box. I felt something wedged in my ear. Leaning over, I dislodged a golden souvenir.

The Perverts

Since childhood I've always been teased about my big ears. They affected my hearing remarkably, enabling me to pick up on sounds or conversations from a great distance. One day I was sitting on a park bench across from a construction site. Two hard hat workers were eating lunch and chatting.

"You have to be bullshitting me?"

"No, listen, I want you to come over and screw my wife."

"Are you fucking nuts? Your old lady is gorgeous. Aren't you poking her enough or what?"

"Sure I fuck the hell out of her every other night. She just out of the blue, told me her pussy was aching for a strange dick. At first I couldn't believe it, but she said she would rather be honest and tell me about it, than to sneak around behind my back. The way she put it made sense, so we sat down and made out a list of possible candidates. Guess who was number one on our list?"

"Well I suppose I should feel rather flattered, but for some reason it all seems kind of creepy."

"Will you do it?"

"I don't know, let me think about it. Now you don't want to do anything kinky, do you? Like swapping wives or a threesome with you or any crazy shit, just a straight old fashioned fuck, right?"

"Right, I won't even watch. I trust you buddy, but don't do too good a job or she might not want me back. Now if you want me to reciprocate by taking care of your wife, I will, but it's not a condition?"

"No, my lady is fine, but thanks for asking. When do you want me to do it?"

"How about Friday night? I'll go bowling and you can tell your wife, you're with me."

"Sounds good."

They ate in silence for awhile. "Let me ask you something?"

"Anything buddy."

"How does your wife like it?"

"What do you mean?"

"You know what positions? Like missionary or doggie style or does she like to be on top like a rodeo queen? Should I eat her pussy for awhile before I fuck her or suck her nipples? Maybe I should bone her ass with a good reaming? She probably wants something different from what you give her, so I guess I shouldn't even ask you? I'll let her suck my dick, good and hard before I fuck her silly. I wonder if I should bring flowers and wine?"

"Goddamn, I didn't know you were so nasty. Stay away from my lady you perverted motherfucker, if you know what's good for you."

He just smiled, as they went back to work. He knew he was going to tap that lady like a barrel of ice cold of Budweiser on a hot summer day.

Pussy Man in Paris

My lady wanted to go to Paris, so after 25 years together we went. Her first language is Spanish, she worked for a French mining co. translating from French to Spanish, when we met. She said her French was rusty, but when we got to the City of Lights she had no problems. Me on the other hand, I asked where the rest room was in a café and they brought me some chocolate ice cream. I had a poetry reading at the English speaking bookstore where Papa H., Picasso, Fitzgerald, and Ezra Pound hung out. It was fun, but no one bought my chapbooks or put any Euros in my beggar cup. The bathroom was a great problem, in the Metro, posters of Carlos Santana and Willie Nelson had lots of Frenchmen pissing on them. I peed on Francis Cabrel's (France's Bob Dylan) and I thought I was in for a gangbang. We descended to the Metro in Montparnasse, where our hotel was located. Billy Holliday had performed there often. I entered the men's room and stepped up to the urinals, hearing female laughter, I turned, still spraying piss. Several cleaning women were pointing at my better than average sized penis, but as my urine splattered their feet, their smiles turned to frowns. I think they had ideas about shoving a mop handle up my ass to clean the mess I made, as I made a rushed exit. When I saw the golden arches of McDonald's, I thought, finally a decent place to defecate. There was a numbered lock on the restroom door, I watched as men looked at the bottom of their food receipts to get the secret code to shit in peace. I figured buying a Big Mac was worth it, I discovered the burger cost 10 Euros which was 15 dollars. I was getting desperate by then and my lady was smiling. I got right behind this dude and kind of stepped on his heels, following him before the door closed in my face. My lady wasn't smiling when I came out and neither was the manager. I guess the security cameras caught my little act. We went to see Jim Morrison's grave, but it was raining and all these worms were squirming about everywhere. The graveyard police said no visitors; they must've been worm lovers or fishermen. Every café we went in had someone with a dog and usually lots of dog crap all over the sidewalk. Outside the Picasso Museum this poodle did a number, I hadn't even seen a horse crap that much back in New Mexico after eating rotten apples. It all sort of evened out I suppose about the dogs. We had to get to airport after our 10 wonderful days and the street sweepers were hosing down sidewalks, streets, café entrances, I saw why no one picked up their dog crap, they had professionals to do it. I also figured out why the Frenchie got upset with me while my lady was shopping in Montmartre and he asked me if I wanted to fuck his sister or wife or mother or tight little brother and when I declined and I asked about his dog. He said, "Fucking Americans."

The Last Night Shift

Stumbling outside from the monster
loud shrieking machine madness, the
black slate floor trying to swallow your
feet to the knees in phobic quicksand,
vote for her or him or me, all crooks

A cigarette, a sip of water in a deserted
parking lot, night, like a workman's
gloves fingers wearing through at the
tips grasping the sun, clutching that
orange red ball to his dark bosom

Quick dozed off leaning against a
concrete wall, he struggled awake
hearing a sound, a lady was playing
trombone with a monkey in a tutu
Ginsberg and Kerouac were playing
bongos, while Burroughs was shooting
and eight ball with Corso, Sanders
passed me a doobie and I felt invincible.

War Everyday Everywhere War Everyday Everywhere

Dedicated to the Australian movie Rabbit Proof Fence about atrocities perpetuated on the Aborigines and the Canadian folks that said America was lucky they let us land our aircraft there after the 9/11 tragedy.

People hate Americans,
they hate McDonald's,
they hate Kentucky Fried Chicken,
they hate Mickey Mouse,
they really hate our drones and nukes

But when they get in trouble
or need money, they all yell
for Uncle Sugar to come running,
they don't worry about teeth getting
rotten and falling out or calluses on
their knees from begging for a handout

All the hawks and doves,
left wingers, right wingers, and righteous,
religion, oil, land, water, pride, and egos

Blood is always thinner than money,
gold is forever heavier than love

Some Americans go hungry,
we cry for our brave soldiers,
that die fighting other countries battles,
killing terrorists around the world

Don't point your fingers and blame us
for your problems or for the freedom we've
created, don't expect us to fill your stomachs

THE REVOLUTION IS NOW ALL WE WANT IS PEACE

Stand up world, pull your own weight,
and leave America out of it for a change.

The Man That Slept With Verbal Hand Grenades Under His Pillow

The Art of War by Sun-Tzu: To fail to take battle to the enemy when your back is to the wall is to perish.

I was having a creative moment
at the typer when the phone
rang, Caller ID read MOD

Thinking great, a call from the
Mod Squad, Peggy Lipton was
sort of sexy and attractive

A woman's voice said, "Hello
we are not asking for money
this year, but your generosity
in the past has led us to believe
that the March of Dimes can
count on you" I thought bullshit

"We would like you to mail ten
letters to your neighbors on S. 59th
spreading the word of our needs"

I said, "You have me at a bit of a
disadvantage, you know my name,
my address, my phone number and to
me you are only a voice on the phone

You say you work for Jerry Lewis' kids,
but I don't know your name, address,
age, description or marital status

But the bottom line is you want me to
do your job for you by extracting money
in a chain letter, Ponzi scheme from people
near where I live, I'd rather donate money"

"Will you send a check?" she asked

"If you can send me a film of you talking
sexy to me, while you are naked, playing
with yourself, I'll think about contributing"

"You are one sick fuck, aren't you?"

"You have no idea, baby, no idea"

The phone rang again, it was a Democrat.

Left Hook Tony

For *Tony Szolwinski -- gone, but never forgotten.*

Tony was 93, he used to box
all through World War 2, he
punched and fought, fists and guns

As he got older, he liked wood
working, building bird houses,
he taught me to find mushrooms,
how to use certain tools, and how
to throw a punch and dodge one

Tony called me and said he had a
problem, he needed my help with,
I came immediately, there were
2 knocked out cold black guys

Bleeding on his kitchen floor, he
said he'd been working in his shop
in the basement and these 2 bastards
were eating his oxtail soup

They'd told Tony, to hit the road
before they whipped his ass,
Tony hit them with a deluge

He wanted me to help drag them
outside and clean up their blood,
before his wife got home from bingo

I called the cops, Loraine, Tony's

wife got home from church and took
one look and hit the ceiling, I tried to

Slip out and make a clean get away,
that's when I was told I was a bad
influence, the cops looked at Tony
and I and we all cracked up laughing.

I Hope that's Pepperoni

Tony the boxer told me
about an Italian joint in
the neighborhood

Back in the '30s, the
owner killed his wife and
chopped her into tiny
bite sized pieces

I made the mistake of
telling my wife and daughter,
now every time we drive by,
my daughter makes stabbing

Motions in the air and squeals
like a dying mouse, to
accompany her invisible knife

Deciding this annoying habit
needed a remedy, I hid a bag
of catsup in my mouth

When we drove by, I bit the
catsup squirting it all over the
windshield, my wife and daughter
and blinded myself

We crashed through their
plate glass window and ordered
a pizza, while waiting on the cops.

Czarnina Thieves

Tony called and said get your
tomahawk and gunny sack, I
asked, what's up, czarnina

I knew it was duck blood
soup, Tony said goose was
better, he said I'll be the
look out and you chop one
Of those big sonofabitch's
heads off, try to save all the
blood, I asked him how in
the hell do I do that

Use your belt and make a
tourniquet, I thought we're
going to jail for damn sure.

The Good, The Bad, and The Ugly

She was the finest piece I'd
ever known, I'd bend her over
the couch and spray lemon oil
on my hammer and drive nails

Grunting and snorting and yelling
pictures falling off the walls,
cats running and screeching
taking shelter from the war

Writing for a gay slanted mag
I wrote, being gay is better
than baseball because you
get to catch and pitch

She commented, you
call that poetry, it's
pathetic, trite, and ugly

While eating French toast
with no place mat, she'd say,
only people in the hood eat
that way, you pig

At night she'd put tree oil
on her neck warts, that stuff
stunk and then she'd want
me to ensnare the warts

With dental floss and garrote
them off, when one got me

in the eye and that side of my
head swelled with infection

I said, arrivederci, she smiled,
and mumbled something I didn't
care I was half way to Italy.

A NYC Salute

After watching 2 dogs
tear each other apart,
we crossed Bowery St..
and saw a handball court
with empty benches

Taking out my map I
tried to figure which way
to travel to end at the
Bowery Poetry Cafe

An old sour faced lady
took a spot and said what
are you looking for, I
told her and she said

There's no such street,
I'm from NYC, I know,
the bird was shy a few
feathers, I hoped a ball
would smack her face

Glancing away, she was
gone, except for a bag, in
it was a bloody middle finger

I looked at my left hand
and decided I had a problem.

Walk It If You Talk It

With mouth agape
in drunken stupor,
rats filling my head

Crunching on me and
me on them, blood
gushing and dribbling

Gagging and retching
bones, tails, slime
fornicating maggots

Spiders and roaches,
flies inside my
screaming mouth

Gnawing at my tongue
and throat and eyeballs
and nostrils and brain

Choking insanely
spitting, vomiting
putrid viscera

I knew I would never
lie to God again about
quitting alcohol.

Gone Amazon

He tried normalcy, but love was
a delicate butterfly, in a tornado,
a facade of yearn and desire

Drink helped to forget to remember,
like ships inside bottles evading
the tedium of a burning world

Inside the circular glass walls knowledge
and serenity lived, oblivious freedom
floating on a precipice of madness

One quiet night he finished a bottle
and had a vision of a ship inside filled
with beautiful Amazon ladies, he
swallowed himself and disappeared.

Soldier Blues

In the army it was all hurry up and wait
Wait ten meters apart from the next soldier
in the chow line or for the latrine so your
enemy would have a harder target to kill

Waiting for ammo for your weapon
for mail call
for your measly paycheck
on a three day pass

Waiting for your monthly cigarette and liquor rations
in formation to be inspected like livestock
for the guard duty list to be posted
for stripes

Waiting to call home and hoping your lover hasn't
taken up with your best friend
Waiting for your nightmares of death to subside
Waiting for reentry back to the world

Praying for a job and not having to live under a bridge.

Dreaming of Paris

Intense sheer walls painted
hyacinth and saffron with
brushstrokes of scarlet sulfur

Searching for silver spoon to
make sotol and datura for sun
tea and going on a magic trip

Dangerous peacocks in a raspberry
sky, green sleeping ducks by the
cattail forest and melodic stream

Rainbow cutthroat trout leaping
for the gnat hatch, fat frogs burping,
loons and cranes on stilts hunting

Thinking about the dancer at the
Crazy Horse in Paris and how I'd
stolen her a Gauguin, she asked me
name, I said Scaramouche.

She Loved Me Because Of Poetry

I am wood, you are fire

I am the beach, you are the ocean
when you're in my arms, nothing is wrong

I'm lying on magic clouds, waiting for you
my love is clinging to the cliff by its fingernails

"My dog ate seven cockroaches,
do you think it will get sick?"

"Naw, I used to eat them squirming
bastards swimming in hot sauce
on tortillas down in Mexico, my cholo
would do the mezcalito sombrero dance"

Six mailboxes, a coyote and a ninja
with three eyes, Hercules, Copernicus
the fear of God and love of Lucifer
dynamite stew and a brass knuckle sandwich

A saber tooth tiger and nine ants
wearing red sneakers and an
electrified rooster monkey

Some search broken dreams and
empty bottles in vain for a past
path of bloody shadows and souls

Lonely phones ring, scream and beg
while sad blue poets have visions of terror
and insatiable ravenous tigers pacing the cage

Francisco Goya's Saturn Devouring His Son
and the Man Eating Mares of Diomedes, she made
her imitation Mona Lisa smile, threw back her
long dark hair and vanished into smoke.

Howling at the Ginsberg Moon

When a car runs over your
neighbors' dog that once bit
a chunk of meat from your leg

When your cat jumps in
the clothes dryer and uses
all nine of its lives

When the hands of time
try to tell you how to live

When the caveman carved
the first wheel and painted a
naked lady on the cliff wall

True revolution is only
found inside your brain
or when the moon smiles.

Speedy Gonzales

Quick's lady inherited a turkey farm,
she asked him to go help until Thanks-
giving and they should make some cash

Fucking turkeys and shit and feathers
were everywhere, he went out in the
field and got toasted, Mary found him

She asked why was he there, he said he
was waiting for the goats to laugh, he
despised turkeys, he rather eat dog shit
she called him a douche bag, he said the

CIA calls it EIT, enforced interrogation
technique, Quick threw some pissed off
skunks in the clothes dryer and split faster
than Speedy Gonzales.

Four Beers a Day

Quick told me he had to blow town
and asked if I'd run his remodeling
crew for a few weeks, I agreed

He had three semi-crazy black men
working for him, they worked hard
in the dangerous neighborhoods of
north side Milwaukee

Paris was a great painter and drywall
man, but he smoked a bit of weed and
crack and liked skeezer dope whores

Samson was super strong, he did most
of the heavy lifting, he carried steam
radiators alone up and down stairs, he
was six foot eight and three hundred lbs.

Willie was Gene's brother, he was virtually
useless, Gene had fallen on his head off
a ladder and scrambled his brains, he wore
adult diapers and drank four beers a day
and always begged for more

Willie would go buy food and run errands
and do a lousy job of sweeping, Quick said
he was on the payroll to help Gene

I found some aluminum crack pipes and
slimy used condoms where Paris was
suppose to be working, Samson called from
jail, he'd smacked a guy upside the head

Gene's sister called and said Willie had drank
Gene's Old Milwaukee, and sold his butt rags
to an old folks' home, I wasn't cut out to baby
sit grown men, I bought a four pack of Colt 45
and chugged them down like fine champagne.

Spanish Harlem

Hot words spewed from
dog stained fire hydrants
in a sweltering Spanish
Harlem July noche

Vatos sat on concrete stoops
comparing nine and ten
millimeter chrome plated
equalizers, pretty mamacitas

Flashed Ladysmith.38's and
legs all the way to heaven,
they all knew a double tap
was a one way ticket to gone.

Honeymoon at Viagra Falls

I didn't think I needed
the blue stiffy pills, but
she insisted, I swallowed

One and waited to pitch
a tent, nothing happened,
so I took another, no results

I crushed and chopped three,
lined them up and snorted
hard like a Missouri mule

Smoke started coming from
my ears, I had a moaner of a
boner for eight days, when

I softened all my hair fell out,
my voice got helium high, I got a
job yodeling at the Grand Ole Opry.

The First Car I Wrecked

My dad went and bought a new baby
blue Ford Galaxie 500, it had a V-8 and
a three speed standard transmission
shifter on the column, he was proud

He would let me play like I was driving,
I would steer, play shift and honk the horn,
one day I discovered the cigarette lighter

I pushed it in and pulled it out and it
was cherry red hot, I thought I wish
I was old enough to smoke, looking
around for something to burn

I noticed the blue plastic shifter knob,
I got the lighter glowing and stuck it to
the plastic, it melted and filled the car
with a stench, I got my ass beat hard.

Eating Televisions

The worm drowns in sun yellow bottle
asleep on the shelf upon a Mayan pyramid
ruin, Jose's eyes fill with death tears forever

Kahlil Gibran says: it's all love baby doll
David Lerner: people hear my poetry and
weep, scream, disappear, start bleeding, eat
their television sets, beat each other to death

Jose swims in the Sea of Tranquility at the bottom
of the Mariana Trench having a mermaid harem,
floating up poems in bottles, never coming back.

My Penis Has No Brain

Gazing into her hazel eyes where
the golden honey flecks swam, I
thought something has to give
With strong suspicions of having
a male clitoris between my ears
that controlled my lusty erections
I'd always walked on the dark path,
following the wind, listening to the
trees, watching the white crosses on
the hill and funerals in the spring
Laying my cards on the table for all
the pretty ladies, popping cherry gum,
turquoise roaches, killing with kindness
Iridescent flies on a bloated corpse, fat
monkeys, beavers in a woodpile, saber
tooth tigers, Eskimo snow ninjas
Just leave the porch lights on, front and
back, if you're lucky I'll stumble into
your neighborhood like Romeo on Viagra.

Nirvana Blues

Seeing a golden finch or cardinal eat from a giant sunflower
hearing Chickenfoot or Los Lonely Boys tear off a riff
watching Romeo Must Die or Lonesome Dove
smelling fresh strong coffee or buttered popcorn
Gazing at Prince play a solo with 3rd Eye Girl
feeling a cat brush and rub against my bare leg
getting a half laugh smile from my daughter
when my lady of thirty years kisses my bald spot.

The Revolution of Love

When my lady is happy, singing
in Spanish and French and I smell
the perfume of Mexican vanilla,
cinnamon, cloves, cilantro, and sage
The cats are purring on the bed
and the snow is melting and chives,
garlic, daffodils, and grapes are
looking at the sun with love
I smile inside I no longer care how
much money I have or owe, or that
I don't drive or my hair is thinning or
that I'm closer to death than life
I put another quarter in the parking
meter, laugh at the shadows and think,
my turn to pull the rabbit from the hat.

the wino and the mermaid

he discovered her sipping
from his stash under the pier
when the bottle was empty
a whimpering sound came
from her neck gills
sea green eyes pleaded for more

the wino turned his pockets
inside out and shrugged
she dove into the surf
and returned with five golden coins

at the liquor store
the owner smiled
giving the wino a bottle
for each coin

moonlight reflected off her scales
as they passed the bottles
silence sat between them

she passed out
the wino slung her over his shoulder
and carried her to his flop

he put her in the bathtub
sitting on the toilet
finishing the wine
he fell asleep and dreamed
he was Moby Dick

Sky Pilots

the golden buds were sticky
like tiny pine cones
they smelled strong and earthy
over a shoe box lid
Antonio crumbled three tops
carefully removing the stems
separating the leaf from seed
he tilted the lid and used
a matchbook cover to roll
the seed away from the flake
taking a gummed cigarette paper
he lined it like a fat worm
twisted it up and licked it
he held it up for inspection
our mouths watered anticipating
the bitter euphoric smoke
Antonio fired it up
took a deep toke and
passed it to me
i lifted the joint toward
my waiting lips
just as all hell broke loose
cops broke down the door
with drawn pistols and shotguns
in hand
spotlights lit up the night
bull horns bellowed
"come out with your hands up"
we felt real fucking dangerous
my lips quivered like
a virgin's cunt as a cop

grabbed the joint and shoved
a pistol under my chin
Antonio and I leaned against the wall
with shotguns against our heads
as his mom's house
was torn apart
they found 6 grams
we were both 16 so we skated
they didn't find
the 10 kilos in our
tree house in the
backyard

Chiapas Lie

TWO YEARS AFTER THE UPRISING
EXTREME POVERTY and SUFFERING PREVAILS

who cares? who listens?

the united states doesn't
crops are still harvested
by slave wetbacks

the RICH have
new ways to FUCK over workers
on both sides of the border
and disregard ecological sanity

the TRICKLE UP theory:
sweat, pain, blood, and misery
means money in the bank
BOTTOM LINE
masked Zapatista women
"negotiate" while
the greedy pig called NAFTA
consumes
land and dreams

buried poisons lie
governments lie
the rich lie

the Mayans and campesinos lie
in graves

The Gordian Knot

The snow melted upon her skin
hot drifting desert sand blown
smooth hungry and beautiful

The two wars inside each person
go on forever, love and hate
the sky always a gun barrel blue gray

After she left all was loneliness and
one can on a table the label read
DEATH, eat it before it eats you.

The Grape Cigar

Mary ripped off the bandage, his brain
tumor was visible, the treatments had
made him worse and she made a blunt

From a grape cigar and some red bud
Columbian, Quick's mouth watered in
anticipation, he told her to put on Tom

Petty singing about dancing the last time
with Mary Jane, he toked hard on the herb
he dreamed of the Louvre and Whistler's

Mother getting out of her rocking chair
and walking like an Egyptian, the Thinker
bumping fists with him and La Giaconda
shedding blue purple crocodile tears.

Noise

A flea on a red hot chile pepper,
ginger on the cream,
ringo on the beatle,
sting on a cop,
a prince, the king,
the slash, the edge,
madonna, a lady,
jimi, the boss,
the kiss, the godfather,
queen, rage against a machine
Hunting hummingbirds with an Uzi,
trying to sleep in a buffalo stampede,
dozing on the tracks before a Santa Fe chief,
it's too late to leave a good looking corpse.

Moose Jaw Blues

Her silk panties blew off
the clothesline as he rode
his chopped Harley by

Smothering his face
in Chantilly lace, asphalt
and a telephone pole ripped
his nuts and nose clean off

The tattooed biker bled
as the paramedic put on
the clean underwear and

Helped herself to his stash
taking a double snort with a $2
bill on the way to Moose Jaw.

Amarillo

My brother called from a
town outside of Tulsa, he
needed my help to remove
some unsavory characters

He knew I'd been in almost
up to my neck in Vietnam and
most of my life, he referred
to me as an overachiever

It felt kind of strange wearing
a star, since I'd always walked
in shadows of good and wicked

My first day on the job, I met
a thief, rapist, and child abuser
all rolled into one, I gave him
fair warning, he pulled his pistol

His hog leg barrel traveled straight
toward me, I double tapped his
chest, his lungs splattered the wall

He was dead an instant before his legs
received the message, finally he folded
like a house of cards, he made a sound
like a broken sick accordion bagpipe

I stayed for a week, I didn't have to kill
anybody else, my brother was relieved
when I laid my badge on his desk,
everyone was rested a lot easier

Pointing my Ford west I headed for
Amarillo and a senorita that could make
enchiladas so good, they'd bring tears
to your eyes and a smile to your belly.

Five Finger Discount

Nasty Jack was a grease ball biker
from near the Mexican border, he
got his name from his Levis being
so stiff, he could stand them up in
the corner awaiting his reentrance

He was always working on Indians
and Harley Davidsons, occasionally
he applied his magic to four wheel ve-
hicles, but he preferred the freedom
of riding in the wind, unless he was

Pulling a big shoplifting job requiring
a crew to cart away the stolen goodies,
his hands were invisible fast, I worked
with him a few times as a distraction
man or driver, Jack knew no fear

I'd entered stores with him and never
seen anything, outside he'd unload
eight huge Porterhouse steaks, three
bottles of Heinz 57 and he'd grab a
rack of fifty packs of Marlboros

Situated right in front of the checker,
he once walked away with two dollies
of booze, one had nine cases of Corona
and the other had top shelf tequila and gin

We never knew what Jack would show
up with next, but he never came home

empty-handed, he wrote a note goodbye and said forget about being thieves, he was going fishing at Boca Chica where the Rio Grande flowed into the Gulf of Mexico.

Crime in Milwaukee

It's rough all over, for blacks
and whitey in blue and out, a
black man was sitting on a bench in
Milwaukee, whitey popo put 14

Bullets in him, he was supposedly
nuts, he grabbed popo's baton, folks
are walking up and down the streets
waiting for Sharpton and Jesse to speak

And Paula Deen to show up and
cook fried chicken and prove she's
not any more of a racist than any
other God-fearing American

Then we have this 20-year-old black
kid that rapes a 101-year-old lady
and wears a dopey grin into court
and he's bragging to the cameras,
saying how famous he is now

A 10-year-old girl on her way
to school was dragged into an
alley and raped by a 26-year-

Old 300 lb. scumbag, he had his
pants down and threatened to
kill the little girl if she ran

Her screams brought people and
the cops arrived, they captured
the animal the next day, but not

Before he molested the girl and
murdered her innocence and purity,
the baby rapist pervert deserves
a slow wretched miserable death.

It Only Hurts When He Cracks a Smile

Quick was hustling nine ball, shooting
with an eagle eye, it was from growing
up on snooker and billiard tables

This dude got pissed off and pulled
out a Saturday Night Special and
shot him right in the ass, his lady
dragged him to the hospital, he felt

Like he was between a dream and a
nightmare, Quick was laying on a gurney
waiting his turn, when they rolled
in a fat heart attack victim, the nurses

Peeled off his shirt, the doc said,
"Son of a bitch, this fucker looks
like a gorilla" they applied the paddles
and turned up the electric juice

His body jumped off the table like a
fish out of water, he was flopping on
the floor next to Quick, they jolted him
again and his chest hair caught on fire

Lucky for him his lady had marshmallows
and chopsticks in her purse, they were soon
having a nice picnic minus the ants.

The Sky Was Larger Than Los Angeles and New York City Having Mad Sex

Angelinos with tattoos made of cocaine,
you could snort right off and watch
the skin change until the next time
they wanted to be a human billboard

Having invented the Magic Straw, I was
richer than Hitler, I bought a crib in the
Pecan Mountains and became a master of
disguise, I was a chameleon of accents

I used the funky names like Fink and Dipstick
and many more unsavory handles, my cook
was missing her thumb, I wondered if I ate it,
I looked up at the blue night and played mandolin

Deciding to give my money to homeless vets,
Native Americans, and the needy, I would ask
them to buy and cremate Mount Rushmore and
turn it into a vast vegetable garden and orchard.

The Last Poem

Quick went from a big fat
rejection slip as a poet to
an overnight success, he was
compared to Dylan Thomas

Bukowski, Pablo Neruda, Li
Po, Tu Fu, Ginsberg, and Corso,
audiences and publishers asked
him how he memorized all of

His poems, he said he learned
them by heart, Quick knew he
was a fraud, a big phony, and
possibly a plagiarist, he'd wake

Up and the poems would be in
his shoes, at first he thought he'd
written them in his sleep, so he
set up a camera to record his

Somnambulism, he saw the cats
moving around, but he never rose
from his bed, he was baffled, Quick
only had to read the poems once

And they were recorded instantly,
he was mystified and perplexed
to the point of sheer madness, his
two cats were the only things that

Kept him sane, the nervous break-
down hit him with a full hurricane

force panic attack, he was over-
whelmed and plagued, as he was

Put struggling into a straitjacket
and led to an ambulance, his cats
shoved one last poem in his shoe
and this is it.

The Panhandle

The snaggled picket fence lay strewn,
ancient teeth in the dustbowl scrub
weed yard, brown yellow sepia washed
clothes hang forlornly on a sagging line

Windblown trees are leaning towers clinging
to red caliche clay and surrendering to the
putrid egg yolk sun, a junky upright piano

A lamp shade and a yucca plant are all that's
left from the Oklahoma tornado, like
the Comanche, buffalo, and armadillos.

Five Times Faster Than Sound

Quick's lady friend Debra Pickleliquor
enjoyed a glass of whiskey or port, so
he went to buy her some ignorant oil
and milk for his cat and hamburger

He had onions, garlic, and rye bread,
when he exited the store it sounded like
a plane was diving from the sky, then
it felt like Thor's hammer hitting earth

Quick turned the corner and saw the
flying machine in flames jutting out the
window of his flop house, he'd miss Ms.
Pickleliquor, her name suited her well

Jimi, Quick's best friend a black cat
was singed but survived, he poured
milk for Jimi and drank some vino,
they slept until the rain came down.

The Blues Jumped Up and Bit Him in the Ass

Refuse to worship gold
diamonds won't fix your soul
when you get to the end of the line
you sure as hell can't buy more time

Winter will overtake you
you'll sleep in a bed of snow
only love can warm your dreams
swim in the sea of know

When sand runs empty in your hourglass
instead of reaching for your family reach
in your pocket it doesn't matter if it's full
you're crying inside drowning in blood

All your blues are turning red.

Onions Make Me Cry

I was reading this book
about a man in Russia
who wrote stories and poems

The KGB came and knocked
him around but didn't kill
him they sent him

To Siberia and stole his
bag containing six onions
then my doorbell rang

There was my lady
bringing me six onions
and a bottle of poison.

The Fortune Cookie

Your weakness is your strength,
the meaning of existence is none,
love is indescribable so is hate

Autumn leaves are dry potato chips,
grape vines are black and red licorice,
tree branches reach like starving children

When you see the sun, dance it will rain,
you can never love more than one person,
take small steps and drink lots of sake.

Dancing With the Queen of Hearts

"Because I'm still in love with you, I want to see you dance again." Neil Young

I write your name
on my heart, I write
your name in the sky

When I smell your
hair and touch your
skin and see your smile
and hear you laugh

I know I live
and love and can con-
tinue in paradise bliss

I want the im-
possible when you
are in my arms, to
stop time forever.

Electric Ladyland

"Dolly Dagger, her love's so heavy, gonna make you stagger."
Jimi Hendrix

Fire alarms screaming cock a doodle dooo,
shadow smoke and stench filled the house,
smelling something god-awful on fire she
was cooking his desert boots in bacon grease

Quick woke up behind the eight ball again,
shacked up with a confidence woman, she had
more swindles than all the beans in old Mexico,
one day Manuela came home with a big chunk

Of Chihuahua cheese, Quick ate so much he got
blocked up like a family of beavers had built
a dam up his ass, he sweated and worked, his
eyes bulged, veins protruded in his forehead

Manuela called her mamacita, she came over
with some flood lights and a douche bag,
Quick jumped in her VW Thing, he called the
dumpster on wheels, put on some Purple
Haze, bullets were flying everywhere, but
none had his name on them.

Nasty Monkey

Monkey got his ass slapped
and dick sucked all the time
he got pussy for a thin dime

Motherfucker liked to listen
to Rooster by Alice in Chains
and Catfish Blues by Skip James

He kissed and licked the ladies
made them laugh and weep
and he never ever went to sleep

Monkey's tail was long and strong
women said it could do no wrong
he ate lots of bananas and sardines
felt patriotic and joined the Marines.

Rasputin's Hedgehogs

There's not a whole lot to do about death but die, her
nymphomania turned Quick into a kleptomaniac, the
little black dog in red panties howled at the blue moon

Quick heard Ginsberg went to Colorado, Micheline
was playing with Skinny Dynamite, Burroughs was
eating lunch nude and practicing his aim, he killed his
woman in Mexico City and only did thirteen days in jail

Kerouac got so pickled he swallowed himself and ended
in a giant whiskey bottle, Bukowski was at the track
checking the nags and ladies, Snyder left for the Far East

Ferlinghetti was eating Coney Island hotdogs, Ed Sanders
was Fugging around playing a musical tie, Janine Pommy
Vega was tracking a serpent, Ray Bremser sold his hat

Wanda Coleman made the voodoo angels fly, Adrian C.
Louis heard the buffalo cry, the tiny white dog in a tuxedo
shimmering with diamonds and sapphires lit a blunt.

Dead Butterflies in the Snow

Your distant eyes
are ice picks now
as chilly words
reduce my world
and I survive

This universe
cannot contain
my sorrow

Don't dare
to breathe
my name
again

I warm my
frozen heart
on your love
letters

And watch your
smile curl
black in
flaming
photos.

While My Raging Typer Bleeds

A zillion ways to die
in a funky junky world

Horses in a snow storm
trapped by mirror ghosts

Shape shifters chasing
vampires into quicksand

Russian tumbleweeds
trouble and bad luck

Sharks eating lions in
the Sea of Cortez

Spanking a guitar like
a naked nasty lady

A chicken fried asshole
of biblical proportions

Cranes sailing above the
Danube on a Siberian wind

Stealing minds and money
in the name of the Lord.

The City of Perverts

Quick told me in Paris
everyone wanted to see
his python, first it was
the mopping ladies in his
fleabag hotel in Mont-
parnasse, then it was a
German woman at the

Picasso Museum, a priest
at Notre Dame, a gypsy
girl in a park, a bum in
the Metro, a man and his
wife in an ice cream shop

At McDonald's near the
Eiffel Tower, they required
a purchase to use the WC,
a Big Mac was $10 to get
the magic code on your receipt

He followed a Frenchie into the
can, the dude insisted on checking
out his junk, Quick said they all
acted like they'd never seen a nice
healthy Americano chili dog.

All You'll Ever Want

My desire is growing and throbbing
and alive, I want you for my ice
cream cone, my sushi smorgasbord,
my velvet glove, my strawberry hills

I want to bury myself deep deep inside
you over and over and over, slow slow
slow honey dripping, fast fast fast jack-
hammer snake slither smooth silky soft

Quiver shiver thrill chill goose bumps,
moan groan back up and hang on, I'll be
coming on strong and so will you, coming
with you coming on on and on together

You can't escape from my sword of love,
my spear thrusting into your soul, we are
one, we are together forever, we can not
swallow our crazy love lust, it's impossible.

Sandman Blues

They kissed upon the mountain until all
the stars became streaking comets swirling
across the infinite heavens and clouds

Quick watched the wind fill her ebony
hair with pink cherry blossoms, but he'd
stared into her empty eyes and cold heart

She was ruthless, without mercy, he gave
her love, to no avail, the sad music wept,
he walked west with the sandman never
looking back, heart shattered and destroyed.

The Eighth Deadly Sin

Quick always kept a secret smile
and a pimp roll in his front pocket

Alexandra sprayed expensive perfume
into the air then nonchalantly walked
into the cloud with a glamorous style

Living in her fire felt like committing
the eighth deadly sin, sleep was on
vacation until you woke up dead

Quick shadowboxed with Diablo
every time her name crossed his lips
sometimes words can illuminate a path
when you feel like giving up the ghost.

Sound of the Sunrise

Born on Elk Creek in the Wichita
Mountains to the Comanche Tribe,
my mother was captured at age nine,
her white name was Cynthia Parker

My father was Nocona, the Lone
Wander, the Llano Estacado was my
home, we lived off of buffalo, using
their skins for homes, until the killers

Came and slaughtered the bounty of
the prairies, we waged war upon the
destroyers of our way of life, at Adobe
Walls, we attacked with Kiowa, Apache

Cheyenne, Arapaho, and Sioux, twenty
eight hunters drove us away, my horse
was shot from five hundred yards, I got
behind a buffalo and was wounded

We fought the Buffalo War again in
Palo Duro Canyon, soon food got scarce,
a wolf howled and ran northeast and an
eagle flew the same direction, I led my

People to Fort Sill, I had eight wives and
used peyote, I hunted with Teddy Roosevelt
and learned about cattle from Charlie
Goodnight, I was last chief of the Comanche.

When Later Never Comes

In the storms of life, the
sky falls apart and lights
the hidden sun, an orange
pomegranate on the indigo

Shadow horizon, leaves
whisper to each other
in a secret language, do they
love the trees that caress and
cradle them through life

Time on earth is a quick
hunt for shelter, you are
my roof, fire, and blanket

Hearts are jigsaw puzzles
with missing pieces, can
you hear the teardrops fall
in a torrid cloudburst.

The Margarita Machine

Quick moved in with a
beautiful woman, she
screamed and bitched
about the movers losing
her margarita machine

Two weeks later when she
found it, she swore the
movers had broken in
and returned it, Quick

Loved her crazy ass, but
got no peace to write, one
night while working on a
poem, she read what he had

(Burroughs cut off his left
pinky at 25, Hitler lost a
testicle in WW1 and farted
so much he got his ass
kicked by his own side)

That sucks she said, that's
not like any birthday card
I've received, Quick packed
his duffel bag and split.

Felony Littering

One night he came back for
his bowling ball, at Margarita
Mama's, he finished a burger,
fries, and a milk shake

The burger bag fell onto her
lawn, she kept Quick waiting
on his ball until, the cops she
called arrived, she insisted he

Be arrested for felony littering,
Quick said the bag wasn't his,
one of the cops offered to throw
away the bag, but she wanted

It to be checked for Quick's DNA,
they refused, she tore the bag
out of the cop's hand and started
looking for a receipt, she

Slammed the front door on all three
men, then jumped in her car and
raced to three nearby hamburger joints
she wanted the workers to pick out

Quick's photo from her cell phone
as a customer or to examine their
security tapes, when the management
refused she started screaming bloody
murder, they called the police

Unlucky for her the same two
cops arrived, they decided her
bullshit had gone on long enough,
they gave her an electricity cocktail.

Boom Boom Lil

She's was a
a wild piece
of ass, she
said, "Just
take your
goddamn blue
pill and fuck
me like a horse"

"I know you
love me like
a motherfucker,
just shut the
fuck up, Lil
I need to con‐
centrate and
pretend you're
someone else"

In about fifteen
minutes a magic
boner arrived,
I worked her from
the front, then
side saddle, I flipped
her over like a dog

I was doing her
right, she started
screaming, then
crowing rooster

style, I said, "What the fuck, Lil are you going chicken on me"

"Nah, when Daddy went to kill a chicken for supper, he always fucked them first to tenderize them" "Well I guess there's nothing wrong with that" I left faster than the Flash with a bad case of athelete's foot and syphilis.

The Ass That Wouldn't Quit

Her ass was fire
Her ass was the sun, the moon, a Tyrannosaurus Rex
Her ass laughed and cried

It could make brave men cowards
It could start wars
It could make rich men beggars

It could make saints into sinners
It could turn water into whiskey
It could make the rain come down

When she walked through the Louvre
It turned the Mona Lisa into The Scream.

Her ass was of biblical proportions
Her ass started playing kazoo, but soon
Mastered all wind required instruments
Including the slide trombone
Her ass made lions and bears roar with hunger

It was the Queen of Sheba doing the Twist
Cleopatra in her prime walking like an Egyptian
Marilyn Monroe in a sheer white dress

All the beauty that Paul Gauguin captured in Tahiti
The marlin that Santiago lost to the sharks
Babe Ruth's grand slam over center field

Her ass was Elvis Presley's blue suede shoes

Jimi Hendrix's guitar from Woodstock
It was Steve McQueen's motorcycle
From The Great Escape

A winning Powerball lottery ticket
The Hope diamond
It was all the words from Pablo Neruda,
Li Po, Tu Fu, and Sun Tzu's The Art of War

A saber tooth tiger, a killer bee, a Spanish fly
A zillion tarantulas crawling up the
Leaning Tower of Pisa

Her ass was the Great Pyramid at Giza,
Chichen Itza, the Taj Mahal, Stonehenge
Her ass was the Dallas Cowboy Cheerleaders
Naked doing cheers on the Great Wall of China

As her fine ass retreated
I poured gas all over my body
And waited for lightning.

Gringo Loco

Quick's sister-in-law in Mexico
City found out he loved coffee,
so she went to her pantry and got
him a bag of special beans from

Chiapas, the coffee was very old
and weak, 20 years later she came
to the U.S. for the first time to

Visit, Quick gave her a roll
of toilet paper and a tube of
toothpaste, his wife and her
sister were not amused

When Quick went south again,
they bought tacos from a taqueria,
there were 2 tortillas wrapped
around the meat, they asked

How he liked them, he said
great except the meatless ones
needed more salt and salsa and
he'd rather eat goat sphincter.

Never Eat Barbequed Seagulls

Set fire to your nightmares, Quick sang,
this one's called Ode to Marywanna or
Death is a Fickle Bitch from Tucumcari

When in doubt trust your heart and don't
pet the jackalope, she's a big bad wolf, a
Comanche on the path of a moonquake

A bullet proof poet with a speed of light
mouth, Quick was a hammerhead shark,
if he quit moving he'd die swiftly.

Supernatural

Sorcery and witchery still flourishes
people need protection, salt strewn
around an encampment helps ward

Off demon attacks, corn meal mixed
with gall of an eagle, bear, mountain
lion, or skunk is potent medicine

Witches live along the Rio Grande,
they steal Mexican sheep and cause
death, beware of shape shifters

Brown and gray corn known as maiz
de brujeria should be avoided, healing
elixers are mercury, Gonzalez herb,
guayuli, and powdered turquoise.

The Tumbleweed

Quick had a crazy girlfriend,
she was a nymphomaniac, which
was outstanding, but she had

A few faults that were difficult
to overlook, she spoke with a
hair lip and stuttered when excited

She had fat hands with pudgy
piggy fingers, her worst problem
was how hairy she was below

The waist, like a gorilla or were-
wolf, Quick said he had trouble
finding her vagina, I told him
he needed a Bush Whacker.

Elephant Tusk Boogie

Fingers chasing each other, notes
pouring forth like champagne

Horns blowing elephant love
feet tapping snapping bo bapping

Bass booming vibrating magic rhythm
crooning words of desire desperation

Monk said his mama looked like a
gorilla and he could never find

Her nipples for all the damn hair
at least he could bend a note on

His piano like a blacksmith making
horseshoes and all the girls smiled.

Six Headed Dog

They stayed together way too long
like a rusty worn out El Camino,
they should've read the writing on
the wall and said it was all over

When she broke the strings and neck
on Quick's blue guitar and fed him dog
food meatloaf, that was the final straw

Quick got on a boat sailing for Cuba,
where the mojitos were strong and cold
and the tobacco sweet, and the women
were vanilla and fantastically beautiful.

Masturbating In a Straitjacket

The goddamn newspaper said
the electric bill was going up
and it would cost more to flush
the toilet, Quick thought holy shit

What's next, there he was sitting
on the porcelain deposit throne
smoking a Mexican cigarette

He heard the doorbell and Poe
yelling, "Get up you lazy bum,
let's go to the cockfights"

Quick opened the door and let him
in, he said, "Man, you don't look
so hot" "No shit motherfucker, you
lined me up blind

With that chick from London,
we went to a British café and ate
some bloody lamb chops then she
ordered spotted dick for both of us

I finally got her home and we
were drinking gin and tonics,
she got drunk and broke my
Chinese lamp, so I got some

Super glue and was putting it
back together, she stuck her finger
in and glued a piece of glass up
her nose, I dropped her off at

The emergency room and parked
my car and an ambulance pulled in
and this crazy fucker was in a strait-
jacket, he jumped out and tried to

Fuck a fire hydrant, I decided it was
time to split" "Are we going to the
cockfights?" "Sure" I got a thimble
for him and a roll of aluminum foil
for constructing my suit of armor.

On Top of Old Smokey

Quickman got his heart broken
by a senorita, so he headed north
determined to join the Mounties

I thought he'd look foolish in a
Smokey the Bear hat, I got a call
from him a few months later

"The Mounties laughed at me, so
I went to a tavern looking for a job,
the bartender asked if I would mind
wearing high heels and licking a few
assholes, starting with hers, I told her
okay if I could rinse them with tequila

One day I was licking this lumberjack's
ass and I looked out the window and I see
two Mounties fucking a reindeer, that's
when I decided to come back home."

Crying From One Eye

Quick sold a mixture he called weed,
he started with some high grade Mexican,
breaking up all the shake, tops, seeds and
stems, then he'd mix in about half catnip

He used a Mr. Coffee grinder on the stems
making them roll able, then he'd fill baggies
with shake, stems, catnip, seeds, and three tops,
his lids looked good and weighed one ounce

Quick was my best friend growing up, I was
making a living off the five finger discount,
there wasn't much I hadn't stolen, we were
quite the rip-offs, when the cops took Quick

My entire world collapsed, darkness smothered
the sun strangling the light from the sky, when
I visited him in Santa Fe in prison, I asked him
If he needed anything and he said, "Never trust

The candy man his treats will make your teeth
get rotten and fall out and beware of losing touch
from not touching, women that cry from one eye,
sometimes the happy ending is at the beginning."

No Blindfold No Cigarette

Vacation in Mexico with my lady
was pleasant except for constipation
everybody spoke of Montezuma's
revenge, it was all the opposite for me

After I insisted on staying in hotel,
so I'd have my own toilet to avoid
embarrassment my bowels didn't
cooperate for five torturous days

At a fancy family dinner of my lady's
family my stomach was growling like
two aardvarks having sex, I made it to
the occupied bathroom, sweat pouring

From me as I clutched the wall, finally
when I got on the toilet, it felt like a
telephone pole crawled out of my sore
ass, that huge log was amazingly scary

I tried to flush it but the damn thing just
swam around a bit and grinned at me, I
needed something to chop it up, pulling
the lid to the tank, there was brick inside

To conserve water, I smashed the monster
into a mash potato consistency, re-flushed,
that shit was sticking to the bowl like cement

Finally I just gave up and faced the family,
my beautiful niece started screaming at her
discovery, I felt like Davy Crockett at the Alamo.

Making the Meat Go Farther

My mama always thought outside the box,
she saw a new product on television called
Hamburger Helper, it looked like dry dog crap

You mixed it with some hamburger and viola,
there was a magic meal in a skillet, my dad
sniffed the air suspiciously, he looked in the
pan and inquired what was stinking so bad

Mama grinned and explained how much money
she saved and how the food would go farther,
dad took one taste, opened the back door and
threw the entire skillet and concoction right over

Our neighbor's back fence, then said, "Honey,
you sure are right about it going far, now let's
all go out for some rattlesnake enchiladas."

Quicksand

Jose's amigos arrived from Austin
in a new 4 cylinder Mustang, they
said it had no pep, they asked him
to destroy it for the insurance money

They harvested 20 lbs of psilocybin
mushrooms, covered them with honey,
froze them, and transported them in an
ice chest, 10 lbs were Jose's if he did

The car, he wanted to strip it and sell it,
but they insisted he blow it up and burn it
he drove out to a caliche pit followed by
his lady and soaked the Mustang in gas &
torched it, later he called the cops

He tried the mushrooms before selling
any, they were strong, sort of like good
acid, but they made him laugh for hours,
Jose decided to go see Iron Butterfly

With a quart of Coors he ate some 'shrooms,
parking his short a few blocks away, the
hallucinations slowed him into snail turtle
motion, his stomach was grizzly growling

Seeing a dark backyard, he dropped a load
and a rat dog kept barking so he used it for
ass wipe, he gazed up at the brilliant sky

It started raining whores and tequila, he felt
thirsty & stiffer than petrified wood, he led

three senoritas to his car and got a bucket to
catch some cactus juice in, looking in the
back seat he saw the stinky little dog

Jose figured he had been adopted, he asked
"What's your name boy?" The dog replied,
"Quicksand, motherfucker and I need a bath."

Eating Dog Without Salt

She went down on me like
an Otis elevator, with a butt
like no tomorrow, I pulled

The pin on the meat grenade,
people in Spanish Harlem and
Hell's Kitchen and Chinatown

Want to hear the angels sing
and the devil scream and take all
your money and bullets and rum

Quick watched Juanita stop traffic
with a drop dead gorgeous body,
her smile fed the hungry, but the

Dog is ice and fire and lives in a
birdhouse above a fire hydrant
waiting to learn how to fly.

Christmas in Milwaukee

Snow kept piling up like dead sheep on an iceberg,
I burned my wooden leg and teeth and started on the
furniture, next came her wooden Buddha collection

Cold wouldn't describe the agony of the weather,
I thought about the J shape of candy canes used
for the celebration of Baby Jesus' birthday

Hearing an eerie howl, the devil came down the chimney
like Santa Claus with syphilis on an eight ball of heroin, he
said he needed to shit, I told him the toilet was out of order

The water was frozen, he stuck his red ass in the sink,
his eyes bulged and he blew a smoke ring, he slapped his
dirty hairy pointed tail up against the wall trying to clean it

Turning around I saw all the candy canes on the Christmas
tree were red and Beelzebub was vanishing up the fireplace
with all our presents, I grabbed his nuts and was jerked up the
chimney like a dead canary in a coal mine, I passed out

The next day, my lady asked how come I was so black and
what happened to her Buddha's, I just shrugged and went to
light a fire with my magic matches the Allumettes Longues
Langes Lucifers, a smelly sulfuric volcano erupted.

Adolf and Elton

The motherfucker with the
Woody Woodpecker hair
screaming into a pink cell
phone in front of the malanga
and yucca root was dancing

Insanely, saying stinking
bitch over and over, I felt like
shoving a turnip down his
pie hole to silence his crap

I bought some mock chicken
legs, wondering what they
consisted of, then I saw the
headlines about Elton's kid

I wrote in my head, in 1944
Hitler had his penis removed
and made into a Nazi swastika
vagina before his trip to Brazil.

The One Eared Dutchman

Jocko's hands shook like a
half jerked off dog shitting
razor blades, rot gut was his

Poison, he'd spill more nectar
than reached his foul gullet, he
used a bar rag or shirttail to
sponge and squeeze his elixir

Down his parched gizzard, the
crack skeezer slouched against
him, looking for crumbs in an
empty eight ball dream

She used to have a walk that
screamed and whispered, I like
to fuck, long ago Jocko would
listen and turn into Van Gogh's ear

A douche bag freak tried to gank
his pile of change and steal his buzz,
a cue stick sang, it was like killing
flies with a sledgehammer

Jocko headed for the beach, the
woman said, good I don't want your
damn pity, he laid in the warm sand
until a mermaid took him home.

Acknowledgements

Fried Chicken and Coffee, Snapping Twig, Blink Ink, Section 8 Magazine, Working Stiff Wrestling Anthology, Silver Birch Kafka and Vacation Anthologies, Rejected For Content #3, Jellyfish Review, Hobo Camp Review, Maji, Across The Margin, Anti-Heroin, Chic, Mush/Mum, Rat's Ass Review, Camel Saloon, Five-Two, Outlaw Poetry, Thieves Jargon, Doorknobs & Body Paint 74, Yellow Mama, Little Raven, Short Fast & Deadly, Horror Sleaze Trash, Giraffes on the Moon, Jurassic Attack, Up Ender Magazine, Deep Water Literary Review, Flyover Country, Queen Anne's Revenge, Roadside Fiction, Visceral Uterus, Busted Dharma, The Commonline Journal, Literary Orphans, Bad Acid Laboratories, Cultural Weekly, Lies People Tell, Mad Swirl, Regardless Of Authority, Dead Snakes, Blue Hour, The Song Is, Jupiter Orgasma, Buffalo Nickels, Grandma Moses Press, Thieves of the Wind, New Coin Rhode University, South Africa, The Otter Magazine, Dryland Literary Magazine, Penny Dreadful Review, Mas Tequila Review, Great Weather For Media, Tales From A French Envelope, Dancing Naked On Bukowski's Grave, Waiting On Nothing, Cacti Fur, Ten Pages Press, Hash and Pumpkins, Naked Fly Cherry Marijuana, Black Dharma Press, Writing Knights, Microbe, Weekly Weird Monthly.

Pski's Porch Publishing was formed July 2012, to make books for people who like people who like books.
We hope we have some small successes.
www.pskisporch.com.

Pski's PorcH
323 East Avenue
Lockport, NY 14094
www.pskisporch.com

www.ingramcontent.com/pod-product-compliance
Lightning Source LLC
LaVergne TN
LVHW051042080426
835508LV00019B/1662